Spiritually
Healthy
DIVORCE

Navigating Disruption
with

Insight &
Hope

Carolyne Call

Walking Together, Finding the Way ®
SKYLIGHT PATHS®
PUBLISHING
Woodstock, Vermont

Spiritually Healthy Divorce:
Navigating Disruption with Insight and Hope

2011 Quality Paperback Edition, First Printing
© 2011 by Carolyne Call

Library of Congress Cataloging-in-Publication Data
Call, Carolyne.
Spiritually healthy divorce : navigating disruption with insight and hope / Carolyne Call. — Quality paperback ed.
p. cm.
Includes bibliographical references.
ISBN 978-1-59473-288-1 (quality pbk.)
1. Divorced people—Religious life. 2. Divorce—Religious aspects—Christianity. I. Title.
BV4596.D58C26 2010
248.8'46—dc22

2010036589

10 9 8 7 6 5 4 3 2 1
Manufactured in the United States of America

Cover design: Jenny Buono
Interior design: Tim Holtz

SkyLight Paths Publishing is creating a place where people of different spiritual traditions come together for challenge and inspiration, a place where we can help each other understand the mystery that lies at the heart of our existence.

SkyLight Paths sees both believers and seekers as a community that increasingly transcends traditional boundaries of religion and denomination—people wanting to learn from each other, *walking together, finding the way.*

SkyLight Paths, "Walking Together, Finding the Way" and colophon are trademarks of LongHill Partners, Inc., registered in the U.S. Patent and Trademark Office.

Walking Together, Finding the Way
Published by SkyLight Paths Publishing
A Division of LongHill Partners, Inc.
Sunset Farm Offices, Route 4, P.O. Box 237
Woodstock, VT 05091
Tel: (802) 457-4000   Fax: (802) 457-4004
www.skylightpaths.com

For Randall,
with gratitude for second chances

Contents

Introduction

Nobody can go back and start a new beginning, but anyone can start today and make a new ending.
—MARIA ROBINSON, AMERICAN WRITER

Radical Honesty:
How Divorce Can Bring You Closer to God

Divorce lends itself to spiritual insight in unexpected ways. The process is never easy and almost always includes profound experiences of pain, isolation, anger, despair, and confusion. Out of these experiences, however, you have a transformative opportunity to see the world in new ways, to reconsider what you value most, and to enter into a more honest relationship with yourself and others. Through divorce you learn more about yourself than you would ever expect and can ultimately flourish in ways you don't anticipate in the darkest moments of separation.

Experiences like divorce tend to rip away your façade and defenses, and call into question what you know or believe. That vulnerability is very painful, but ultimately can bring you to a place where your spiritual life can gain strength and insight if you are open to it. In the midst of feeling lost, you can find a new path forward, which brings you to a better place.

If you are reading this book, you are likely acquainted with the process of divorce. You may have already been through it, you may be immersed in it right now, or you may be considering it. Your spiritual life—however it manifests itself—will be intimately tied to and affected by your divorce. What I hope is that you will be willing to explore with me how your spiritual life might be developed and enriched through the divorce experience. I hope you will use this book as a guide to empowering yourself through the divorce experience, to promote your own spiritual and personal evolution. In spiritually healthy divorce, you do not dismiss the pain involved in the breakup of a marriage, but navigate through the journey of separation to arrive on the other shore as a better integrated and more connected person.

While it may be hard to imagine how the painful, scary, and debilitating process of divorce could enrich anything, I am here to tell you that it can happen. The pain you're experiencing now can bring transformation to your future if you figure out how to let it teach you and lead you toward greater authenticity and wisdom.

Each of these chapters is a way of sharing with you what I have learned from my own professional and personal experience. As an ordained minister, I have worked with individuals considering divorce, as well as those moving through the process. As a social scientist, I have conducted research on how divorce and spirituality intertwine and affect each other. Each time I speak with people about their divorce, I hear a unique narrative, some filled with more pain than others, some with greater insights or lessons learned, some with greater or lesser realizations about themselves and how they connect to the wider world.

While each of these stories is unique, they share some common elements. These commonalities form the basis for this book. I believe that in listening to one another and sharing our experiences, we help to light the path that makes moving through this landscape easier and less isolating.

Personal Experience, Universal Lessons

The book is also born of my own experiences as someone who has lived through divorce. Like every bride (and groom), I assumed my marriage would last for my lifetime. I did not enter into my marriage lightly and I never thought that divorce was an option or even a possibility.

Along with thinking that it would never happen to me, I also believed that I would be shielded from divorce because I was a spiritual person. In my hubris, I thought that because I was ostensibly in touch with life's deeper meaning I knew more than other people did and I could steer clear of divorce. What I found instead was that even though my spirituality did not protect me from divorce, once my marriage did break up, my spiritual life came to buoy me through the process. Following my divorce—and as a result of it—my spiritual life became more rich, complex, and authentic, and I developed a more honest and loving relationship with myself, God, and the communities I engage in. Eventually, I entered into a healthy and happy second marriage.

Seeking new paths is part of every spiritual journey. If you are pursuing a spiritual quest or journey, you are looking to discover and explore what makes your life meaningful, whole, and purposeful. As you gain insight, perspective, and knowledge, you cultivate a more complete understanding of life. This is a key part of healing from divorce. You may be tempted to see divorce as a moment in the journey of your life, something that you will eventually "get over" and then you will be able to "move on" with your life. While these things do happen, this is not how I approach divorce.

By contrast, I see divorce as one of many threads that make up the tapestry of life. That means that the thread of divorce is woven into you and becomes part of you. It changes you and never completely leaves you, but its legacy is more than the remorse of a broken marriage. Rather, the key question becomes this: How will it change you? For better or for worse? Can you take the lessons learned here and use them to deepen your spiritual life and bring greater wholeness to your spiritual self? I believe the answer is emphatically yes.

But getting there is not a simple process. Divorce is the second most emotionally wrenching event an adult can experience (the first being the death of a child). This is because it tears your life apart to the very core. Not only does it bring change and havoc to your emotional life, but it also shatters your financial, professional, familial, and spiritual lives. It touches all parts of you. This book is designed with that reality in mind. To cope with divorce in a spiritually healthy way means exploring it in all of its complexity and considering all the ways it challenges and rearranges your life. This means that there is no quick fix. There is no way to go around this experience. The only way to create a new path for yourself is to forge ahead into the new landscape, no matter how strange, frightening, or hostile it seems. This book will help you navigate this new landscape carefully and consciously so that you can make your way forward in the most spiritually healthy way possible.

Mapping the Journey

We start by looking at spiritual life and consider what constitutes healthy spirituality. Throughout this process, you will keep spiritual health as your ultimate goal. By embracing the concept of healthy spirituality and keeping that uppermost in your mind, you will develop greater self-honesty and authenticity, making the entire process more meaningful and more spiritually uplifting.

After determining what spiritual health looks like, you can consider what it means to create a spiritual map for yourself, how a spiritual guide may assist you in the process, and how to avoid spiritual cul-de-sacs that lead to dead ends.

Divorce affects every aspect of your life. As a result, it is difficult to discuss and explore in a systematic way. But to make your way through this landscape, you have to take each piece of the process and examine it on its own. When you do that, you gain a far richer understanding of how this event is shaping you. With greater understanding comes greater control and a greater sense of having power over your own life. So after you consider the tools for navigation in chapter 1, you will look at your own interior life—specifically your self-perception and self-esteem. In chapter 2, you will focus on how you define and understand self-perception, how it is connected to spirituality in your life, and how it is disrupted by divorce. The third chapter is devoted to self-worth and the damage to your self-esteem brought on by divorce. By probing how self-esteem and spirituality are connected, you'll learn how you can reclaim your self-esteem in spiritually healthy ways. Following self-examination, you move outward, looking at your actions and behaviors and your relationships with others (chapters 4–7). Finally, you assess your relationship with God (chapter 8) and how the ground or source of your spiritual life is affected by divorce.

What Is Healthy Spirituality?

The development of healthy spirituality takes time and effort. Most religious traditions hold that healthy spirituality requires self-reflection and, often, self-sacrifice. In this new landscape of divorce, reaching the horizon of spiritual health will be your primary goal. For our purposes, building a healthy spiritual life refers to attaining particular states of being, such as integration (vs. compartmentalization), humility (vs. hubris), self-acceptance (vs. self-denigration), compassion (vs. indifference or disparagement), responsibility (vs. self-justification), and self-control (vs. personal excesses in behavior or speech).

A healthy spiritual life also encompasses the experience of connection or awareness of the sacred reality beyond yourself (God) and the ethical demands of that connection. A consistent connection to the life of the Divine can expand your heart and lead you to experience awe, wonder, a sense of oneness with the world, and a posture of gratitude.

Each of these aspects of spirituality figures prominently in considering the profound role divorce plays in your life. Let's start by looking at the ideal of integration.

Integration

In the integrated life, all the various aspects of your personality and values, behaviors and desires, habits and aspirations are in alignment with one another. There is no sense of division within yourself, and your values and actions reflect consistency and congruence. Radical honesty and transparency to yourself as well as to those around you usually characterize integration of the self. Integration is threatened by secrecy, dishonesty, and fear.

Humility

Humility also requires radical honesty with yourself. Yet humility is often mistaken for becoming a "doormat." Instead, genuine humility comes when you are able to openly acknowledge your faults, failures, and shortcomings while also acknowledging your gifts and abilities. Humility is the honest assessment of the self and includes recognizing your own limitations in terms of knowledge and experience. It also reflects an understanding of the inherent flimsiness of social status and the human reliance on external trappings to define worth. Humility stands in contrast to hubris, which is visible when human beings are overly confident of their own power, status, abilities, or correctness. Humility is difficult because it can conjure up feelings of guilt and shame, and you may have to admit that you have been wrong. We will explore humility in greater detail later on and witness how embracing it can be liberating.

Self-Acceptance

This works hand in hand with humility. Oftentimes when you move toward taking responsibility for your failures or shortcomings, you feel such shame or guilt that you become convinced that you are worthless and unable to offer any good to the world. Healthy spirituality does not elevate the self higher than it deserves, but it also does not crush the self or deny its inherent worth. Reaching a place of self-acceptance can take years. Divorce is especially threatening to that sense of self-acceptance because the emotional power of the situation tends to undermine self-worth and can push you into your absolute worst behavior. Depending on the circumstances of the divorce, it can also crush your ability to believe in your own value or worthiness. Self-acceptance is a state of spiritual health, while self-denigration leads to hopelessness, the inability to act or move forward, and even, at times, a paralyzing depression.

Compassion

Kindness to yourself and others, a spiritual virtue associated with all major world religions, is an essential component of successful relationships. It stands in contrast to the disparagement of others or indifference to their plight. Compassion implies empathy, a complex emotional response learned early in life. Approaching another person with an attitude of compassion is easier when you already know and care about that individual. Interacting with all human beings—whether friend or enemy—with compassion is a much more difficult undertaking. This is especially true when you have been emotionally or physically damaged by another. A life of compassion is intimately bound with humility, self-acceptance, and an integrated self. In its highest form, compassion can be expressed through the gift of forgiveness. How to reach this point is one of the most challenging parts of your spiritual journey.

Responsibility

As a truly responsible person, you claim your own ability to make decisions and then take ownership of your decisions and actions. You are unwilling to blame others for your mistakes and you clearly see your own role in conflict and suffering. This is in contrast to self-justification, in which you find more and more elaborate ways of justifying your actions in order to escape the burden of owning them. When you take genuine responsibility for your actions (good or bad), you claim them as your own and bear the consequences.

Self-Control

Finally, spiritually healthy individuals practice self-control. In one sense this means being able to read a situation and respond appropriately and in an effective manner. Maintaining self-control also means recognizing that not all desires and cravings are positive (even if they feel good) and that through sacrifice you can achieve liberation. While self-control does not require the stifling of creativity, it does call for an understanding that spontaneity and impulses are neither wrong nor unspiritual. In fact, for some, the road to spiritual health may involve a release of some aspects of self-control so spiritual responses flow freely. But, ultimately, as a spiritually healthy person, you learn how to navigate and move within relationships in a way that preserves freedom and joy while also respecting and maintaining boundaries.

In cultivating spiritual health, you'll find that these elements relate to and intertwine with one another. Moving toward greater humility, for example, usually also means moving toward greater self-acceptance and often, greater compassion toward others. These are not boxes to be checked off, but dynamic and complex realities that you sometimes master, but may have to relearn and practice again and again.

The narratives throughout this book will show you how a variety of individuals have moved toward these spiritual goals, away from them, and back again. The spiritual life is, ultimately, one of ebb and flow—the key is to maintain an overall forward motion.

While spiritual health encompasses all these elements, which happen within you and within your relationships, you must also recognize that spiritual health also deals with your connection to God. Coming to understand your relationship with the Divine is a worthy, lifelong quest.

Even if you grew up in a faith community, you'll need, at some point, to reclaim the relationship as your own and make your own decisions about who God is to you, and what and where you are being called to within that relationship. In my work with individuals going through divorce, often the most confusing and painful part of the process is coming to terms with how divorce disrupts, damages, or challenges their relationship with and concepts of God. You'll learn how divorce undermines the divine relationship and how you can be healed and renewed.

The ultimate goal is to arrive at the other side of divorce as a spiritually healthy individual. This is not an easy path. It will require intensive self-reflection and honest answers to difficult questions. You might also have to rethink and reconsider some commonly held perceptions or attitudes. But achieving spiritual health is worth the work if you are able to grow through it into a more compassionate, humble, loving, and self-accepting person. Even if the rupture of divorce is the impetus for this journey, it can be a stepping-stone to a better life and a more authentic, connected spirituality and relationship with God. Out of something devastating can come a greater good—something of ultimate value.

( )

Beginning the Journey

Navigational Tools

A journey of a thousand miles must begin with a single step.

—LAO TZU, TAOIST PHILOSOPHER

When I first met Ruth* she was an attractive and successful businesswoman in her early fifties who had been divorced for over ten years. Ruth's divorce, however, remained a driving force in her life more than a decade later, and her story illustrates just how deeply divorce can cut into your sense of self, your relationships with others, and your view of God.

Ruth was a devout Roman Catholic when she got married soon after college. Her religious tradition taught her that marriage was sacramental and a lifelong commitment. She loved her husband and they raised two children together. Both she and her husband had high-paying jobs and their lives were comfortable. Ruth remained active in her church by regularly attending worship services and felt she had a strong faith.

---

*All names are pseudonyms.

Nothing had challenged her faith particularly and she drew great comfort from it.

So it came as a profound shock to her when, after twenty years of marriage, her husband left her. Ruth was devastated. Her faith and her entire understanding of her own life fell into disarray. She was plagued, even years later, by a deep and relent-less confusion. She simply did not understand, she told me, why God had done this to her. When I questioned her about this per-ception of God, her response was poignant. Ruth exclaimed, "But I did everything right! I went to church and I raised my children in the church. How could this happen if I did every-thing right?" As I grew to know Ruth, I saw how the divorce had damaged her self-esteem and eroded her faith. Her self-perception became one of a confused victim. She had difficulty establishing and maintaining new, meaningful relationships. While she attended a new (Protestant) church sporadically, she never regained her previous sense of spiritual intimacy with God. She felt deeply betrayed, not only by her former husband, but also by God.

Ruth's story stands in sharp contrast to that of David, who was also raised in a religious tradition and married soon after college. He, too, raised a family with his wife. David understood that his marriage was meant to be permanent and believed that this was what God had asked of him. Yet over time David began to see things differently. He was deeply unhappy and felt belit-tled and rejected by his wife. More and more, he found himself pulling away from her and the relationship. Counseling and dis-cussions with their rabbi did little to help. In his prayer life, he came to see that God was calling him out of his marriage. In order to become the person God called him to be, he needed to separate himself from his wife. David's faith grew through the experience of his divorce and he went on to work with others who struggled with faith and life decisions within his religious tradition. Further, David's relationships with others took on new depth and stability and his self-perception grew in positive directions. He came to feel closer to God after his divorce than he had while he was married.

The experiences of both Ruth and David exemplify how deeply divorce can alter, challenge, or change a person's self-perception and interactions with others. It can also undermine a person's established faith. The experience of another woman I worked with, Ellen, illustrates the same principle in a slightly different way.

Unlike Ruth and David, Ellen had never been involved with a faith community. She had what she thought was a stable marriage, built on mutual respect and shared interests. While she occasionally wondered about exploring the spiritual side of life, her husband was not interested and neither of them believed it was necessary to the health or stability of their marriage. The marriage went sour slowly; both Ellen and her husband experimented with drugs and sank into depression. During Ellen's eventual divorce, a friend introduced her to neopaganism and she found herself drawn to alternative forms of worship as a source of strength and empowerment. She ended up joining a Unitarian Universalist community and now assists with services while she continues to eagerly explore her understanding of the Divine. She came to see the connection with the sacred as a critical part of her self-understanding as well as necessary for deep relationships with others.

In their disparate responses to divorce, all three of these individuals illustrate how deeply spirituality—a complex, multilayered reality—underlies human life. This reality figures in your psychological self as well as how you comprehend or relate to the sacred. All three found that divorce challenged, affirmed, or rearranged their relationships with themselves, others around them, and their concept of the Divine. Delving into this trifold reality is a critical component of understanding divorce and spirituality.

The Dynamic Triad: Self-God-Others

As the stories of the Ruth, David, and Ellen show, divorce has the potential to disrupt, damage, change, and reconfigure your spiritual life. That is, it speaks to your understanding of what your life means, what your purpose in life may be, how to live your life authentically, what has ultimate value to you, and the kind of life to which you are being called in the future.

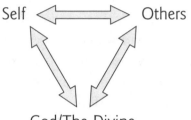

My understanding of the spiritual nature of humanity is graphically illustrated in what I call the dynamic triad of Self-God-Others (see the diagram above). This may appear on the page as deceptively two-dimensional and static. But the dynamic triad is better imagined in three dimensions, as a pyramid rather than a flat triangle. What this complex rendering reflects is that you are constantly in relationship—with God, with yourself, and with others.

Your relationship with others, for example, affects how you relate to or understand yourself. Your relationship with God can have a significant impact on how you relate to and act toward others. This is a dynamic and complex reality and within these relationships are embedded your most deeply held values, beliefs, and aspirations. Recognizing and exploring this triad offers one way of considering the spiritual impact of divorce, and all three aspects of the dynamic triad can be seen in Ruth's, David's, and Ellen's stories. As you work through this book, you will move from the "self" to that of "other" to that of

"God." You will consider how divorce affects each node and how this, in turn, impacts the others. Think of it as a compass or a gyroscope that you carry with you as you move through the space of divorce. You will explore how it can help you maintain proper orientation when you feel lost or confused.

If you consider the dynamic triad, you can see how divorce causes disruption in each of these relationships. It touches the very deepest parts of your self-perception; it can radically alter your connection with others; and it affects how you look at or relate to God. Because humans are social creatures, relationships make us who we are. From the time you are an infant, your life is shaped and supported by other human beings. Your sense of self, worth, and purpose—all are molded by your relationships and with how others respond to you. Marriage is one of two relationships that hold the highest honor in our society (the other is the parent-child bond). When a marriage breaks apart, whole lives are shattered. I saw personally how divorce damaged all three nodes of Ruth's dynamic triad. She lost her sense of connection with the Divine, she lost a sense of personal value and esteem, and she lost her ability to relate to others in a healthy and life-affirming way. Yet for David and Ellen, while the process of divorce brought rearrangement to all three nodes, it also brought healing and renewal.

Navigating with Spiritual Maps

In some ways Ruth remained lost in the terrain of divorce while David and Ellen made their way through. When I went through my own divorce, I was struck by how often I described the process to others in terms of being "lost," "swept out to sea," "finding my way," "not knowing where to turn," or other journey-related terms and phrases. It became clear to me that divorce requires navigation, and the resources for navigation are often unreliable or missing altogether. I found the same references to travel, journeying, and navigation when working with others going through divorce and have since come to see how desperately we need help with the navigational process. So often the reference points on which we have depended vanish or become unrecognizable.

This is especially true when it comes to spiritual life. While many individuals find help and guidance in secular psychological resources, it can be difficult to find any resources within religious communities or at spiritual centers. This is surprising, given the substantial impact of divorce on people's spiritual lives. My hope is that the dynamic triad can function as a compass or gyroscope to offer you insight into and perspective on the spiritual process of divorce.

You have the ability to craft a spiritual map for this journey, a map that will help you move in a positive direction, avoid painful routes, envision where you want to end up, and find the best ways to travel. The process of map making is critical for a simple reason: your previous map has failed you. Ruth and David had spiritual maps to their marriages crafted by their religious traditions and their own personal backgrounds. Both believed in the maps they had for marriage. They believed they knew where they were going, how to get there, and what they would encounter along the way. So the experience of divorce was deeply disorienting; their previous maps no longer provided direction and their compasses no longer worked. The mapmaking process takes on deep significance when you realize that your previous maps no longer offer the direction and the guidance you once believed they would.

This is not a superficial exercise and you may find it harder than you expect. The map you make for yourself will need to be adjusted and revisited, but it can provide you with much-needed direction. Just as maps are important when you're embarking on an actual journey, they are important in divorce as well. They help you move through the process consciously. By this I mean they enable you to think clearly about your goals and consciously push forward, always aware and reflective, in contrast to moving through divorce by simply reacting to what is happening to you. Engaging in some spiritual map-making can assist you in being proactive instead of reactive. The dynamic triad is very useful as you begin constructing your spiritual map and seeking new directions for your life.

The idea of a spiritual map can be envisioned in the following way. When it becomes clear that a marriage is ending, you can think about how you want to proceed and what your expectations are for your own behavior. Simply put, one of the first things you might consider for a spiritual map is what you want to avoid. Then you could reflect on what route to take to do your best to avoid those things. For example, one of the behaviors you might be most concerned about is your own use of language and how you talk about your spouse with friends, family, and people who have known both of you for years.

You might also be concerned about how you talk to your soon-to-be-former spouse while going through the legal and financial processes involved in separation and divorce. You might decide to make a commitment to avoid the use of disparaging language, even when you feel justified in using it. This would show respect toward your spouse, even though the world of divorce is often marked by disrespect, anger, frustration, and deep emotional pain. The route you could take to avoid this part of the landscape of divorce could include deliberate prayer, discussions with a close confidant, journaling, or a variety of other activities. This reflects one side of the dynamic triad, that of being in relationship to others. It also demonstrates a positive, proactive orientation that allows you to nurture your own spirit by avoiding the negativity and pain that you inflict on yourself by using disparaging language.

This is not meant to sound simplistic or easy. In fact, these types of decisions are difficult to make and difficult to carry out. You will often revisit and rework the map. However, the exercise enables you to move forward with more consciousness about your choices and with a greater sense of control and objectivity. Throughout this book we will explore further how various behaviors, perceptions, and attitudes can be addressed by considering your spiritual map. We will use the dynamic triad as our compass or gyroscope to maintain a spiritually healthy orientation while engaging in these exercises.

The Compassionate Mirror

Another tool to help you navigate the landscape of divorce is the spiritual guide. For some of you, this person will be a trusted friend or mentor; for others it might be a clergyperson or a psychology professional. The role of the guide is not to agree with you or to commiserate with you, even though both of these tasks have their place. The guide functions as a compassionate mirror, allowing you to see yourself honestly, reflect on your own actions and thoughts, and maintain a sense of balance or perspective. It is crucial to assign at least one person to serve in this role for you if you are going through a divorce. What a profound difference it might have made for Ruth in her journey. The goal of spiritual health is a difficult one when your own life has been broken apart. You need at least one person who can lift you up, speak the truth in love, and grant you much-needed perspective. Sometimes multiple people can fill this role, with various people serving as guides for brief periods, even if they are unaware that they are fulfilling this role. In subsequent chapters we will hear about some of these guides and how critical their role is to maintain your spiritual health.

Spiritual Cul-de-Sacs

Finally, one of the most important navigational concepts in the book is the idea of spiritual cul-de-sacs. For those not familiar with the term, a cul-de-sac is a circular end of a road. Employed in suburban housing developments, it is different from a traditional dead end. A cul-de-sac is usually round and houses are often built around the perimeter. It is a place where you can drive in a circle, but cannot go anywhere (except back out again). Avoiding spiritual cul-de-sacs is a core goal of this book and of the navigation of divorce. In this book, when we refer to a cul-de-sac, we're talking about an emotional, behavioral, or cognitive pattern in which people get stuck, often moving in circles and without making any progress. Once again, Ruth can serve as an example here. At the time I knew Ruth, she was clearly caught in a cul-de-sac and could make no forward progress. She was trapped in a perpetual cycle of confusion and betrayal, spinning her wheels and gaining no traction—spiritual or otherwise. Her gyroscope was off balance and she could not navigate toward a space of spiritual health or rest. Some examples of cul-de-sacs we will explore include victimhood, resentment, and demonizing a former spouse.

The cul-de-sacs we will discuss are often stopping places on the journey through the landscape of divorce. Getting caught up in them is understandable and often justified. But they are not the goal of the journey. My experience in working with those going through divorce has shown me again and again that cul-de-sacs are incompatible with spiritual health. A major point of your navigation will be learning to distinguish your true destination from a spiritual cul-de-sac.

If you have come this far, you are ready to take the next step. Let us move into the dynamic triad and start exploring what this landscape of divorce looks like.

Questions for Reflection

1. Considering the metaphor of navigation, how would you describe your own journey through divorce?

2. When you think about the idea of a spiritual map, what are some things that you hope to avoid?

3. Who has served as a spiritual guide for you in the past? Who do you feel might serve as a compassionate mirror for you? Why?

4. How has your spiritual life been manifested in or through your relationships with God or with others?

5. As you begin this journey, how would you describe your hoped-for destination?

( )

Seeing Clearly

Fostering Lucid Self-Perception

The most valuable thing you can ever have, you already have, for it is your own special life. Allow it to unfold, in each moment, in all its beauty and wonder, and be the real living fulfillment of who you are.

—RALPH MARSTON, AMERICAN
INSPIRATIONAL WRITER

To fully explore the landscape of divorce, you must begin by looking at yourself and the roles you played as a single person within your family of origin, your religious community, and your culture. These roles tend to fall by the wayside when you get married, replaced by a new set of roles. With divorce, these marital roles—and rules—are supplanted once again as you make the shift from couplehood back to singlehood.

The first of these shifts—becoming a spouse—can dramatically alter your identity when you, as a solitary individual, become part of a larger whole. Consider the candlelighting ceremony so popular in contemporary marriage ceremonies: The two flames become one as the participants light the unity candle. In some renditions of this ceremony, each individual extinguishes his or her candle once the unity candle has been lit. The message of wedding ceremonies in all faith traditions is very clear: The two have become one. In the wake of this experience, your self-perception changes to reflect your new status as you acquire the powerful title of wife or husband. Women who change their names upon marriage can find themselves with yet another public display of unity as their identity shifts: Miss Jane Doe becomes Mrs. Thomas Smith.

In profound ways, these changes can influence your identity in general and your self-perception in particular. In Western culture the monogamy-based, romantic ideal assumes trust between partners, accountability, and mutual affection. Through subtle or overt messages, the cultural ideal spells out what it means to think of yourself as a good wife or a good husband. Being trustworthy and loyal are obvious assumptions, along with the idea that you are in this for the long haul and you have committed for life. You also tend to prioritize your self-perceptions around marriage and the general assumption is that you are leaving your family of origin to make a new family and the new family should become the new center and focus of your life.

If you add children to the mix, you gain even more layers of identity: you become not only a spouse, but also a parent. Children can reinforce the sense of unity with your spouse. Biological children are formed as a result of the act of physical intimacy by two people. In the adoption process, children are usually chosen, planned, and anticipated together with your spouse. Stepchildren can be part of this new family, too, often resulting in deep emotional bonds. Each of these complicates the identity picture. Rearing children adds yet another dimension to your self-perception, freighted as it is by the cultural and personal expectations of what it means to think of yourself as a good parent.

The bottom line is that marriage deeply transforms your self-perception. Who you think you are when you are single becomes significantly more complex, multifaceted, and value-laden when you get married. You become emotionally invested in your self-perception as a married person and all the beliefs, values, and behaviors that it entails.

Divorce ruptures all these aspects of your identity at their very root. At its worst, you come to believe that everything you have invested in has been false and you may be startled to find that you no longer know who you are. Even the best or most amicable divorce can push a person to question who she has been and who she will be in the future. How you think about yourself can change dramatically or be challenged in disturbing ways. One client, Frances, speaks eloquently to this sudden awakening:

> Oh, I guess I thought I had a charmed life ... growing up had its very serious problems, but I just trusted myself, my abilities, my commitment, my brain, ... Immortal youth. So, the divorce was a kick in the head. This wasn't supposed to happen to *me*! And it did. So then I began to get real. I think I have learned, starting then, that life can happen to anybody, and no matter what you think or do, it can all fall apart and we need to be there for each other. I am a more gentle, patient person now and that began for me with the divorce. I discovered in therapy, which followed the divorce, that I had been an angry, judgmental, arrogant person. Seriously, I was just so sure of myself. I needed to get that knocked down a notch or two, or forty, in order to be a real person.

During my own divorce, I, too, came to see my dark side. I struggled daily with how I seemed to be becoming a person I did not even like, much less one I admired. I had always thought of myself as straightforward and honest. Now, suddenly, I found that in the midst of my hurt and anger I was becoming manipulative and impulsive. I behaved in ways that did not mesh with my self-perception as a compassionate, patient, and strong person. Instead, I began to think of myself as weak and volatile. I also struggled mightily with accepting my new role as a divorce statistic and, even worse, being a failure at something at which I had always thought I excelled: human relationships. The end of a marriage can shake up all your assumptions about yourself—what you are capable of and what you can actually control. Michael explains how his divorce changed his self-perception:

> Before my divorce, I believed that I was the kind of person who would be committed to my marriage regardless of the circumstances. After thirteen years of marriage, I realized that I had married someone I did not love and I could not live with this person because of her refusal to get help for her personal problems stemming from her childhood, which were seriously affecting our marriage. I was very disappointed in myself and experienced a great deal of guilt for initiating my divorce. I thought that my knowledge, wisdom, education, and determination could create enough change in my ex-wife and the circumstances to make our circumstances tolerable. I came to understand that a "marriage" does not make a relationship healthy. But healthy relationships can make a marriage healthy.

This shaking-up process can also expose our biases and our own pride. Jon, like Michael, came to see this and recognized how the stigma of divorce can have a lasting effect on self-perception.

> I used to think that divorce only happened to other people. And despite my desire to be compassionate, I think I viewed divorce as a failure of one or both partners. I thought that with enough dedication, my own marriage

could never fall apart. And then, when divorce seemed to be the only gracious way for my ex-wife and me to move forward, all of a sudden I was one of those other people. It took months—maybe years—for me to accept that I was a divorced person.

Divorce can tear or fray multiple strands of your identity. The most obvious strand is that of husband/wife. For Barbara, a woman in her forties, divorce was eye-opening and frightening because it exposed how heavily she had relied on her spouse and her role of wife for her identity.

> Before my divorce I saw myself as above that sort of thing and was somewhat judgmental concerning others who were divorced. I would not have dated a divorced man while I was single. I felt like that was something that would never happen to me. I was fairly secure in my marriage. While the marriage was not perfect, I felt safe because I believed my husband felt the same way about divorce that I did. I saw myself as a "good" wife and mother, a responsible person, able to run a household, hold a good job … While I still believe most of those things, divorce did change my view of others who are divorced. I no longer believe they are automatically in the wrong or not trying hard enough.

Besides the identity of spouse, your understanding of yourself as a good parent may also be shaken to the core by divorce. Guilt, anger, manipulation, fear, and so many other emotions come into play.

Not only may you question your role as a parent, but you may question your role as an adult child. In working with individuals facing divorce, I often find that people struggle with feelings of being a bad daughter or a bad son because they have

failed at a relationship. Not only do they feel they have let themselves down, but they have also let down one or both of their parents. These feelings may be especially strong if your parents are
still living and married and if they have invested heavily in the
marriage (emotionally and/or financially). Mallory struggled
with this for some time.

> Going through a divorce made me feel like I was a com-
> plete and total failure. I carried lots of shame. It was
> something I never imagined that I would go through.
> Prior to that time, I was the "good daughter" ... and
> when I couldn't keep up the plastic-happy façade any
> longer ... my parents got really angry with me. I was ruin-
> ing their entire world in some ways ... I knew they were
> hurt and angry and they thought that I was a failure.

Sanctification and the Pain of Divorce

Mallory's pain was exacerbated by her involvement in a faith
community and her understanding of herself as a Christian at
the time of her divorce. This faith dimension may further com-
plicate the sense of identity loss or rearrangement by manifest-
ing itself in what Kenneth Pargament calls *sanctification*.
Pargament, a professor of psychology at Bowling Green State
University, explains that we come to identify objects, places, and
relationships as sacred. The process of sanctification involves
the perception that various objects or ideals or experiences (such
as a chalice or a wedding service) can take on divine character
and significance.

Sanctification happens in most faith-based wedding ceremonies, regardless of religious tradition. In my own wedding ceremony, I can still recall the moment that the pastor took our
hands, wrapped them in his stole, and proclaimed loudly, "What
God has joined together, let no one separate." There was no doubt
whatsoever that my wedding in general and my vows in particu-

lar were meant to be perceived as holy and sacred, promises to be respected and honored because of their connection to God.

Sanctification is expressed in different facets of your life in various ways. It can affect what you invest your time and money in and what you work to protect and preserve. Consider, for example, how often people think of their role as parents as holy, believing that they have been entrusted with children as a gift from God. A sanctified object may serve as a springboard for spiritual emotions (awe, wonder, praise) as well as a resource to draw on in times of need. For many, marriage takes on a sacred character and purpose, providing us with our greatest support and shelter from the world's harshness—a place where we experience some of the deepest human emotions. Physical as well as emotional intimacy with our spouse, for example, are often viewed as sacred and can be windows into the divine life.

On the flip side, the power of sanctification means that when something you hold sacred, like marriage, is lost or damaged, you experience profound suffering. Self-perceptions and identities formed and shared within marriage break apart, not only on the cultural or social level, but on a spiritual level as well. This is what Pargament refers to as *desecration*. The experience of desecration injects a caustic and painful edge into the divorce process by undermining your self-perception as a faithful participant in your religious tradition.

Letting God Down

Although divorce is acknowledged within all major religious traditions, it is never viewed as desirable. For most faiths, divorce represents what God does not want for humanity: brokenness, suffering, betrayal, grief, and anger. Understanding that your marriage is sanctified or sacred means that divorce is the breaking of that faith and the turning away from what you believe God wants for you. In essence, you may come to believe that you have let God down.

This was how I felt, and it was one of the most difficult aspects of my divorce to talk about with friends or family. After all, here I was, an ordained minister, presumably someone who was close to God and knew what God wanted for my life. I was a "good Christian"—not perfect by any means, but I thought I had a good grasp on the way God worked in my life and to what I was called. And, when I got married I believed that my marriage was God's will for me. All the connective tissue of faith had become part of my identity and self-understanding.

Like many people, I believed that mine was a holy marriage. But the reality turned out to be much more complex. I came to see that I had not been very good at discernment before I got married and I had not been spiritually honest with myself or with my husband. Yet much of that is hindsight. And this is one of the great pains of divorce—learning that your knowledge of yourself and of your partner may actually be quite limited, if not false. This humbling moment can break you down, but it can also free you by showing you the limits of your own power and knowledge. Mary's story speaks to this.

> My separation and divorce made me feel that I was not the kind of person I used to think I was. I had always thought, "I'll never get divorced" and there was actually a great deal of pride in that belief—I thought I somehow "knew more" or "knew better," and thus could protect myself from divorce. So I thought of myself as "not the type of person who gets divorced"—whatever that means. Obviously, I had some pride issues and thought I was better than others. So in time I came to see that I was just as flawed as other people, and just as capable of screwing things up. Eventually, this had a liberating effect, but at the beginning I was in denial that this could be happening to me.

Mary found liberation cultivating a healthier spiritual identity, one that acknowledged her ability to make mistakes and cured her of seeing herself as better than others. In a similar way, I have stopped focusing on what it means to think of myself as a "good Christian"; I now prefer to think of myself as a disciple, someone who is still learning and still in training.

The Cul-de-Sac of Victimhood

Sometimes following divorce you can get mired in the task of the rebuilding your identity. You get stuck or find yourself making no progress—just traveling in circles. One of the most tempting cul-de-sacs on this journey is the one that casts you as a victim. The temptation here is to claim a new identity as the blameless injured party. This can seep into your sense of self without your even being conscious of it. Other times, you might consciously claim the title like a flag and run with it. You protest to your friends and family, "I did nothing wrong! I'm the injured party here!"

Why is this particular cul-de-sac so tempting? Simply put, you are injured and feel you have been wronged. The image of victim may be the only self-identifier you are able to grasp in the midst of your pain. It may also be an identity foisted on you by others who have empathy for you or are your self-appointed protectors. The identity of victim gives you a place to rest in your pain. It can also confer benefits. If you're perceived as a victim by those around you, you garner sympathy. The sense of care and protection offered by those close to you can be comforting and empowering. I understand this particular cul-de-sac all too well.

I found it empowering in an odd way when others saw me as a victim of my husband's selfishness, callousness, and disregard for me. People had sympathy for me and in some ways that felt very good. But when I was alone and could reflect on the situation honestly, the little voice in the back of my mind became louder. That voice said, "It's not all his fault." And when I was truly honest with myself, I knew that each of those words—*selfish, callous, disregard*—could be said of me at times as well. For me, claiming to be the victim was simply dishonest.

Further, portraying yourself as a victim may also help you to feel righteous and thus boost your ego, which may desperately need it. Claiming the mantle of victim is understandable when you are going through a divorce that seems unfair or brutally one-sided. And certainly there are those who actually are victims in a relationship, as in the case of an abusive marriage. But even in the worst of situations, being a victim cannot be the ultimate resting place for your identity because it will not allow you to move forward or make your way successfully through the landscape of divorce.

Casting yourself as a victim is overly self-focused. While it is important to concentrate on yourself in a healthy way and claim your own voice, there are limitations and your self-focus must be balanced against your relationships with others and with the Holy. The dynamic triad reminds you that you are not the center, with all other relationships and issues orbiting around you. Instead, you are part of a complex web of relationships that demand your attention and your respect. You are not the only one who has been hurt and wronged. But to insulate yourself within the role of victim allows you to draw all the attention to yourself. This is a form of spiritual selfishness.

Victimhood is spiritually unhealthy because it is grounded in past events and thus binds you to that past. Being a victim defines you by something someone else did to you in the past, making it difficult for you to choose and shape your own identity for the future. It saps precious energy as you spend time rehearsing and recounting the hurtful deeds of your former spouse.

Finally, it limits your ability to see beyond yourself—your own pain and helplessness are your primary concerns. Your identity can be reshaped within the dynamic triad by reaching out toward God and toward others. Spinning around this cul-de-sac does not allow this to happen. You cannot reach out to others and move beyond yourself (much less toward the Divine) if you are focused only on your own wounds.

Holding on to Hope

The ultimate goal of this journey through divorce is spiritual health and authentic living. Your self-perception is one of the places to begin as you start drawing a new spiritual map. There are a number of ways to approach this task of healing. Some of these suggestions are specific actions or behaviors that you may find useful. Others are habits of mind that can make your journey go more smoothly.

Before considering what you could do to help yourself, it is wise to check the condition of your heart. When you stand in this new landscape and look to the horizon, what do you see? Is it dark? Bleak? Frightening? Or is it hopeful and filled with potential? This is not meant as a look-on-the-bright-side platitude. The role of hope in this journey is critical. Years ago, when I worked with a woman in the parish whose husband had died, she repeated a phrase to me that she'd heard from a friend. When she asked her friend (who had also lost her husband) if the grief would ever end, her friend replied, "It doesn't get better, but it does get different." In many ways, divorce—the death of a marriage—mimics the experience of the death of a spouse.

This phrase—it doesn't get better, but it does get different—has stayed with me and I think it speaks to a realistic view of grief. That is not to say that we will never feel better after suffering through a divorce. In fact, the majority of people find themselves happier and living more authentic lives after divorce. But in the throes of the pain and the confusion and the chaos of change, it is helpful just to keep reminding yourself that things *will* change. Things *will* be different. The experience of grief, anger, sadness, guilt, hopelessness, or any of the other emotions you feel will shift in time and you can come through this process and out the other side as a strong, healthy, and positive person. Ellen, whose grief at the dissolution of her marriage was intense, finally experienced this transformation herself:

> Getting divorced made me realize I am a much stronger and more resilient person than I thought I was. I made the change and not only survived, but flourished. As a result I feel more confident and empowered, and I have a wonderful sense of power that comes with making my own decisions and living my life the way I want to. I think I'm a happier and more balanced person now, and as a result I'm a better parent, a more creative worker, and a more loving, caring friend and companion.

Ellen's experience is one that you, too, can embrace, as you travel through this landscape. Believing that a better life awaits you is crucial to coming through the divorce experience spiritually intact.

Respecting Time

Most of us are rather impatient when it comes to healing. When we are sick, we expect our illness to pass quickly, especially if we have good medication. As Americans, we live with impatience much of the time, always seeking faster ways to get where we want to be, whether it is a physical or a mental destination.

While serving in the parish, one of my parishioners was diagnosed with a brain tumor and she was scheduled for surgery just two days after the diagnosis. She had always been a very active woman and was deeply relieved when she learned that the tumor, which was quite large, was also benign. When I saw her in the hospital several days after the surgery, she was already able to walk halfway down the hall and back on her own. I found this impressive and told her so. She remarked that when she got halfway down the hall and had to turn back, she had complained bitterly to the nurse that she could not go further. The nurse had laughed and said, "Relax! You just had *brain surgery!*"

This story always makes me laugh because I think to myself that I would have probably acted and felt just as my parishioner had. But if I would be impatient after having my head cut open, how much more impatient was I when my heart was cut open by divorce? I, too, expected rapid healing and assumed that I could force the process of recovery. I do not know why we are so impatient, but I do know that if you try to run too fast through this new landscape you might just trip and fall and hurt yourself even more. Or you may end up running into a cul-de-sac.

Divorced people often lament to me, "I should be over this! It's been a year!" Yet I have found that three years is a better time frame to use. Some people require more time, some less. But don't expect too much of yourself. This is a process of rearranging and redefining your life after a major transition. Whether you're coming back to someone you were before your marriage or constructing a new version of yourself afterwards, it takes time for new patterns to emerge and for changes to settle in. Giving your heart the time it needs to heal is also a sign of respect for yourself. Truth is, most of us never truly "get over" our divorce. The landscape changes and our lives go on, but the previous marriage and the experience of the divorce change us. They become part of us, and they shape who we become in the future. There may not be a getting over, but there can be a getting on. Robin's words are especially poignant in reflecting what it means to respect time while on this journey.

After twenty-eight years of marriage, it is a bit terrifying to step off this cliff of indeterminate height. It is also a bit freeing. Most of the time I feel pretty good about myself—not always—but most of the time.

To be authentic, to be my true self, to not live a lie any-more—those are the goals I am slowly working my way toward. I am not fully there yet ... Most days I feel pretty confident about the outcome of this, but there are plenty of dark nights of the soul.

I *was* a wife who tried to keep the peace. I tried—turn-ing myself inside out—subverting myself to keep that peace. I *am* evolving into the person I think God created me to be, not walking away from those that I love, but hope-fully bringing them along with me in love and relationship.

Recognizing Grief

One of the consistent surprises of working with those going through divorce is how seldom they recognize what they are experiencing as grief. There is a great deal of anger, there may be feelings of betrayal and rejection, and there may be fear, anxiety, and a deep ambivalence about the future. All these may be man-ifestations of grief. Perhaps it is hardest to see grief when you are in the throes of anger and rage. You want the suffering and the pain to be over and you want this person out of your life. However, while wanting a clean break is understandable, mak-ing it happen can be a bit more challenging.

Divorce means the rending of a profound emotional bond that is forged through the attachment process. *Attachment* is the technical term used for human bonding, and attachment pat-terns and experiences begin when you are an infant. From the design of your brain to the role of hormones in your body, you are built for attachment and bonding. In marriage you come to experience the deepest expression of human bonding (outside of parenting) as you mesh your life with that of another human being. So when that enmeshment tears, you suffer the pain of grief as your individual self begins life without the one with whom you shared that life (however imperfectly). Put simply, the deeper the attachment, the greater the grief at the loss.

Besides the loss of a relationship and the attachment that defined it, you also grieve for the loss of dreams, hopes, plans, assumptions, and beliefs. In reflecting on her own divorce, Mallory called it the "death of a thousand dreams." Part of the deep investment in marriage is the belief that you can plan your life around your union. You will have children, you will have dogs, you will have a house and a yard, you will travel, you will retire together, and you will build something of significance. However these dreams manifested themselves in your marriage, you will grieve for them in your divorce.

There comes a time when new dreams grow out of the seemingly barren soil of divorce. But until that time comes, I encourage you to allow room for grief in your life and respect it. Honoring grief can be more difficult than it appears. The process is even more challenging when those close to you do not understand why you are mourning, especially if you were treated badly at the hands of your spouse. But grief is natural and it is normal. Even though you may want to say to yourself, "Oh, get over it! I'm better off without him!" you need to recognize that your emotional system will require time for that to actually happen.

As you grieve the loss of your marriage, you should avoid the quick fix of new relationships and being redefined by a new person. Even if you move out of a marriage into another relationship, you might consider taking at least some time to be on your own. Aloneness is the ability to be comfortable with your own company. Admittedly, this can be challenging, especially when being with another intimate partner can soothe your pain and bring you a sense of comfort that is difficult to find alone. Reaching out to others and to God can bring you to new understanding of who you are, but it cannot be done out of desperation.

Finally, it may be helpful to recognize the spiral nature of grief. It rarely progresses in a straight line and this can be frustrating and confusing to us. Time passes and you may feel upbeat and focused, and then suddenly you'll be reduced to tears or to guilt or to anger by someone's offhand comment or an object that sparks unbidden memories. Grief moves in spirals. You revisit places you have already been (such as anger toward your spouse), but now you have new perspectives and new insights. Even with the new insights, the emotional triggers can still pack a powerful punch.

Ten years after my own divorce, if I come upon a note written by my former husband tucked in the pages of a book, I may be struck by overwhelming sadness. While I recover quickly and move forward, the emotional reality of divorce has a very long shadow. Respect it. And be patient with yourself when you come upon emotional anniversaries (such as your former wedding anniversary). Respecting time goes hand in hand with recognizing grief and its power.

A brief word about the connection between grief and depression: Almost all the people I've counseled have acknowledged feeling depressed either during or sometime after their divorce. This is one of the dark sides of grief. Among other symptoms, depression may manifest itself by an overwhelming desire to sleep; struggling with distraction, the lack of focus, or initiative; losing interest in everything around you; developing irritability; and a short temper. Depression may be linked to anger, and may, for some, reflect the turning of anger inward against the self. At its worst, depression may bring you to thoughts about suicide. The experience of depression needs to be taken seriously; it requires medical and professional help. What this might look like will be explored in greater depth in chapter 4.

Practicing Your Spirituality

The best place to cultivate hope, respect time, and allow for grief may be through your spiritual practices. Allowing space and time to care for your spirit can have a deep effect on your healing from divorce. Karin's divorce opened her to a new world and to a place she could now explore on her own.

> My bad marriage and graceless divorce made me real-
> ize that I *was* a spiritual person. There was no room for
> spirituality (or for any emerging part of me) in the mar-
> riage. I can't say it was a credit to me that I left it—I
> really felt driven to go, and threatened if I remained—
> but the process of leaving gave me a new sense of
> myself as being called to something deeper, something
> grounded in my own questing, spiritual nature. In the
> aftermath of the divorce—and its consequences—I went
> back to church and found validation of my instincts for
> spiritual search and faith community—a place for tears,
> questioning, deep sharing, self-exploration, all the parts
> of myself that had been forced underground in the
> marriage.

You may nourish your spiritual life within a particular religious tradition. Attending worship services, participating in prayer, and reading holy scriptures can reorient you and give you new perspective on your identity and who you are called to be. Karin's exploration of the spiritual life following her divorce opened avenues for deep conversations and profound reflec-tions. These, in turn, affected her self-perceptions, as she describes below.

> Ultimately, it was going back to church that most helped
> me to reshape my self-perceptions. Early in my renewed
> churchgoing, I had an opportunity to preach on "History,
> Feminism, and the Church" on a women's Sunday in my
> small hometown church, which helped me to think
> through and attempt to integrate those dimensions of my
> personal, academic, and spiritual life. Church also

offered, from the start, a community of faithful, generous, and caring folk, who—unlike my marital circle and
my grad school peers—were concerned with the ultimate, important issues and passages of life. Early in my
renewed churchgoing life, I participated in a still-memo-
rable retreat and an equally memorable "open sermon,"
which invited intimacy and exploration with others on a
spiritual path and built lasting supportive, spiritual
friendships. I also found a wonderful community of
friends, loosely affiliated with my church, which spon-
sored a singles group in which I met my new life partner.

Traditional versus Nontraditional Spirituality

While traditional religious practices are helpful to many (especially prayer, which will be discussed in the next chapter), others
find hope and healing in nontraditional sources of spiritual life.
Spending time in the woods or on the beach can open your spirit
and grant you new perspective, as can time spent with animals
or in the garden. For Ellen, creating works of art with her
divorce as a theme proved tremendously healing to her spirit
and helped her to reclaim her identity as a creative person. For
her, artwork and creativity were sacred realities.

You might find it necessary to leave the traditional site of
your spiritual life (church, synagogue, mosque) for a time. For
some, this separation becomes permanent and the life of the
spirit comes to be nurtured through new activities and commitments. For others, the journey away from church proves surprisingly healing as they find a new appreciation for the complexity
of the spiritual life. They could, eventually, return to the house
of worship—although usually in a new community or denomination. Moving from one spiritual community to another raises the
question of how to reclaim your identity as a spiritual being or
how to make peace with feeling as if you fell away from what
God wanted from you.

First of all, the spiritual life requires the long view. This means that just because you may be resistant to your tradition or faith life now does not mean that you will remain resistant in the future. Anger, frustration, confusion, and grief can throw up some powerful walls and this may include barriers in your relationship with the Holy. Secondly, if you are experiencing an aversion to your faith tradition or practices, then listen to your heart. By asking yourself some questions or discussing it with a trusted friend, you may be able to pinpoint the root of your concern. Find a place to explore what you are experiencing with a spiritual director, at a retreat center, or in a divorce support group hosted by a faith community. You may need to step away from your former faith life and explore some alternative means of nourishing your spirit for a time. Divorce can deliver a terrible blow to your faith identity. As it turns out, people who go through divorce are the most likely to fall away from religion altogether or, at the very least, change denominations.

The important message here is that your life within the dynamic triad of God-other-self calls you forward into a life of the spirit, however you come to know it. The spiritual aspect of life is a critical component of your identity and to ignore it or turn away from it may lead you to a shallowness and avoidance of the deeper mysteries in your life. It may also lead to a false sense of recovery. Your healing cannot be complete and you cannot map out your new direction if you ignore or deny this part of yourself.

Writing Your Life

Journaling can be an effective way to work through the identity crisis that can result from divorce. Writing encourages self-reflection and metacognition (thinking about your thinking). It can help you recognize patterns and it can allow you to be honest in ways you may not be able to do when speaking about the situation with another person. Writing is an excellent way to reflect on your new horizon and to "talk yourself through" the kinds of changes you want to make as you move forward. It should allow you to explore and open yourself to new ways of thinking and self-perception. It should not end up as a bullhorn from the cul-de-sac! Challenging yourself, not bullying others, should be the goal.

You also should be realistic about what writing can do and what it cannot do. With the rise of journaling recently, many see it as a therapeutic tool that can cure whatever ails you. As a person who has kept a journal since I was twelve, I usually agree with this statement. However, writing is not for everyone. Some feel more comfortable talking through reflection questions than writing about them. You may find yourself drawn to writing poetry or snippets of phrases rather than long and richly contoured descriptions of your inner life.

At a 2010 conference on the intersection of faith and writing, memoirist and educator Leslie Layland-Fields reminded would-be writers of what is involved in "writing into our sufferings." She noted that not all writing is therapeutic and that "writing into affliction can bring its own affliction." That is, it can hurt to write. The purpose of writing about our pain should be to seek greater understanding while recognizing that understanding may elude us for some time. Writing can be one of the best ways to press your experiences for meaning. This means reflecting on them in a sustained, conscious way, in order to wring out what is valuable. You need to discover the hard lessons inherent in your suffering. Layland-Fields noted simply, "Pain is holy with meaning." Writing on your own or in a group is one way to explore that meaning.

Exploring New Roles

Identity is multifaceted and composed of a variety of elements. You are more than the simple titles of wife or spouse. You have cultural and spiritual identities that you may not yet have explored. Janice worked for years to unearth who she was out-side of her marriage. The process brought her to a new sense of identity:

> I have moved from viewing myself in terms of my rela-tionship to my husband to being able to think of myself as an individual. To be able to live my life as I want to. Instead of understanding myself as a suburban house-wife, I now see myself as a bisexual mother, friend, and would-be professional in a field of my choosing.

The prospect of exploring new roles may be terrifying to us or it may be exhilarating. Ellen talked to me about problems in her marriage for years before she finally decided to go through with the divorce. The identity role she feared the most was that of "single mother." To her, it carried cultural stigma and implied negative judgment. Not only was she afraid of being judged by others, but she also worried that she would not be able to bear the weight of the responsibility within this role. However, after her divorce was finalized and she moved to a new home, Ellen found her relationships with her children had shifted toward greater communication and honesty. Part of that change occurred because Ellen sought out others who were single moth-ers and looked to them for advice and as role models. She has redefined herself as a mother and no longer considers the title of *single parent* an embarrassment or one to fear.

Exploring new roles can be as serious as returning to school or as simple as taking a cooking class. Divorce may give you a chance to renew your acquaintance with yourself by researching your own family history, reclaiming abandoned cultural prac-tices, visiting or reading about a variety of religious traditions, starting a yoga practice, or learning how to dance. Identity is so complex that you may forget the other roles you play besides that of spouse or parent, such as a sibling or friend. Sorting through your identities through divorce may grant you the opportunity to reclaim some of those roles as well, reestablishing relationships or mending fences from your past. All of these are valuable and significant endeavors.

The Compassionate Mirror: Reflecting the Truth

As you map out your new spiritual direction, I will return in each chapter to one of the most significant aspects of the healing process—the compassionate mirror. The compassionate mirror is one person in your life who will stand beside you throughout this process and offer you a place to talk and a place to reflect. This should be someone who will be unfailingly honest with you while remaining compassionate—someone who can speak the truth in love. For many of you, this person will be a professional: a therapist, spiritual director, healer, pastor, rabbi, and the like. This person is crucial to your healing and recovery.

I learned many lessons while going through my own divorce and in working with others as they go through theirs. The most important of these has been the need for someone to walk beside you. I also learned to recognize the difference between commiseration and genuine self-reflective seeking. There is a place and a time for commiseration. You need it and it helps to clarify what is happening in your life. We all need friends who will sympathize with us, gossip with us, and affirm that we are better off without our spouse.

However, commiseration alone can become self-defeating. It can allow us to remain trapped in simplistic explanations and overgeneralized opinions. It can also lead us into a cul-de-sac of victimhood. If we seek genuine spiritual growth and health, then we must resist the easy path. Commiseration is easy. Sharing with your friends the most recent debacle with your ex is easy. Looking closely at your own role in the failure of your marriage is much harder. And coming to accept your responsibility for actions within the marriage can be harder still. This is why you need a compassionate mirror—someone who can show you the truth about yourself (as a decent mirror should), while still holding you in love and affirmation.

Questions for Reflection

1. What are some of the threads that have been woven into your identity? Consider family (close and extended), culture or geography (ethnicity, places where you have lived), spiritual or religious beliefs/rituals, education or work experiences, and physical characteristics. What do the different threads look like? What is the pattern that emerges?

2. Are some of these elements more important than others? Which ones, and why?

3. What threads were added to your identity when you got married?

4. How has your self-perception evolved or changed in your marriage?

5. Which threads were broken or frayed in your divorce? What aspects of your identity still remain or are valuable? What might your new "tapestry of identity" look like down the road?

6. What activities, rituals, or experiences have been helpful in reconfiguring your identity?

7. Who has served as a compassionate mirror for you in the past?

( )

3

The Gift of Humility

Building Healthy Self-Esteem

You, yourself, as much as anybody in the entire universe, deserve your love and affection.
—SIDDHARTHA GAUTAMA, FOUNDER
OF BUDDHISM, SUPREME BUDDHA

Underlying spiritual health is a strong sense of self-esteem based in the ability to recognize and embrace your own value as a person. Primarily emotional in nature, how you value yourself is a critical component of selfhood. Ellen found that trusting in herself instead of the judgment of her former spouse was the key to regaining her self-esteem.

> Getting divorced improved my self-esteem, as I learned that I truly can trust myself. When I was married, I was made to feel like my decisions were questionable, that my sense of intuition was weird, and that my upbeat and confident attitude toward life was arrogant. I know for sure now that those things are not true, that I make good decisions, that I have a strong sense of intuition, and that being confident and upbeat creates positive energy around me. It feels great!

As with self-perception, self-esteem can be damaged, even destroyed, by divorce. Current research on self-esteem focuses on a two-pronged model. In this view, healthy self-esteem arises from the intersection between a strong sense of personal worth and a strong sense of personal competence. Neither one of these is sufficient on its own to produce authentic, healthy self-esteem. So what do personal worth and personal competence look like in day-to-day life?

Personal Competence and Personal Worth

Competence is best understood as physical and social skills or abilities, such as the ability to run a household, work at a job, care for children, or maintain numerous friendships. Competence is also a process: You become more competent depending on how much the activity means to you and how personally invested you are in succeeding at it. In most cases it involves practice and a degree of mastery. You feel competent when you complete a difficult task, whether it is cooking a complex meal, playing a challenging piece of music, or getting through a public speaking gig. It is a sense of accomplishment and reflects an affirmation of your capabilities.

Worthiness, on the other hand, turns on the personal meaning of your actions. You experience a sense of worthiness when you behave in ways that align with your values and beliefs. While worth stems from acting in congruence with your values, it also involves a sense of belonging. You come to view yourself as a worthy or valuable individual when others around you accept you for who you are. This acceptance by others (complete with faults) and the resulting sense of belonging are the bedrock of self-esteem.

The Roots of Self-Esteem

Where does self-esteem come from? In general, it is formed early in life through the response of others to you. How much and how consistently you are touched, fed, cared for, and interacted with as a baby and as a child influences the formation of self-esteem. And while a foundation for self-esteem is laid in childhood, it remains a potent part of your selfhood as an adult as well. In adult life, self-esteem usually comes from a combination of acceptance by others (as opposed to rejection), living virtuously (as opposed to being racked by guilt), having or wielding some measure of influence (as opposed to feeling powerless), and achieving goals (as opposed to failure). All these adult sources of self-esteem can be undermined through the experience of divorce.

Self-esteem is linked with your spiritual life as well. As a spiritually healthy individual, you can reflect honestly about your choices and yourself; be authentic in your relationships with others; and pull disparate parts of your life together into a meaningful whole. Spiritual health also encompasses your understanding of and relationship to the Divine. For a person of faith, one of the key parts of believing that you are a worthy person is the belief that you are accepted by or belong to God. Your self-esteem will suffer if there is a disruption in that relationship or if you believe that God no longer accepts you. When your self-esteem is damaged, living out healthy spirituality becomes very difficult. Feelings of unworthiness hamper your ability to be open and honest in relationships. Believing that you are bad or worthless interferes with your ability to trust yourself to make and carry out good decisions. And low self-value can lead you to hide your heart and life from communion with the Divine.

How Divorce Affects Self-Esteem

Self-esteem is an internal, felt reality, which can be affected by the response of others around you, especially people in your inner circle of relationships and intimacy. The reactions of others to your choices, behaviors, and feelings can alternately boost your spirits or flatten you. The internal aspects are often closely tied with the external, so that your sense of competency and/or worth can be influenced by a single negative or positive comment from someone on the outside. Usually, the comments from those closest to you carry the most weight. Here the impact of divorce on self-esteem can be seen most clearly. All of the individuals I have counseled about divorce can readily provide examples of devastating words addressed to them by their former spouses. These words can damage you on a deep level because you usually take the judgments of those close to you very seriously.

Regaining Self-Esteem

Self-esteem can be affected by divorce in two very different ways. On the one hand are those whose sense of self was lost, disfigured, or hidden during marriage. For these individuals, divorce allows self-esteem to reemerge as they reclaim their own inherent sense of self-worth and competence. However, this does not mean that divorce is any less difficult, emotional, or heartbreaking for these individuals than for anyone else. Rebuilding or reclaiming your sense of self calls for marshaling tremendous emotional resources. It is an arduous journey, requiring time and reflection. I refer to people who regain their sense of self-esteem through divorce as *regainers*. Janice, Karin, and Ellen all fit this profile. A sense of liberation and recovery suffuses the words of Janice and Karin. Janice writes,

> Separation and preparing for divorce have actually increased my self-esteem. While I do enjoy positive feedback from friends and coworkers, ultimately I am the one responsible for feeling good about myself. I can walk in the world, and express myself in situations with more confidence than I ever have before.

Karin's words demonstrate the feelings of renewal and rebirth that can emerge from this experience. Her new sense of herself is palpable, and she draws strength from having reclaimed her authentic self.

> I wouldn't boast that I was proud of myself for walking out, but it really shaped my own sense of what I was called to be and could/should value in myself—a person of faith, a feminist, a scholar, a lover of cats, a serendipitous housekeeper, a hanger-of-pictures ... all the things I had lost or subdued while I was married. So ... yes, leaving and the subsequent divorce restored my sense of self-esteem.

Remaking Self-Esteem

For others, divorce deals a sharp blow to self-esteem, and the self is broken or deeply damaged as a result. Their internal sense of competence and/or worth are hurt, leading to feelings of disempowerment. I refer to those individuals as *remakers*, since they need to remake or reconstruct their sense of self-esteem, often with very different components than those present during the marriage. Mallory's experience is especially poignant in this regard, and she has worked hard to remake herself.

> I struggled with the sense of failure when my marriage fell apart ... unlike any other failure in my life. I felt ... that I would never get past it. I fell into a depression that I thought might never end. I slept a year away. It took years to rebuild my self-esteem ... to think I might be OK.

In this case the damage went further, in that her divorce took away a central aspect of her self-esteem—her voice:

> Before my divorce I used to sing publicly a lot. It took nearly five years to begin to sing again. To sing publicly took even longer. Today I still shed tears during praise

and worship songs at church ... it is a slow process to
accept the love of Jesus ... to feel like I am OK. Now ...
after ten years ... I do know that I am OK.

Sometimes the damage comes from hearing the judgment of
others (such as your spouse) and being found wanting. This can
be especially hard when you have no other significant voices to
balance the one that comes from your spouse. This was the case
with Cynthia, who writes,

> I had allowed my self-worth to come from and be dic-
> tated by my ex-spouse. He was very angry by my decision
> and lashed out repeatedly, telling me I was a bad person,
> unlovable, unworthy. A bad mother. I really struggled
> with this. It was hard to be around other people. I can
> remember dreading school and family functions because
> I felt that everyone else must be judging me.

This kind of emotional damage can raise profound questions for
you about what you might have done differently in your marriage. Jon's confusion and sadness come through clearly in his
remarks and the questions he poses.

> Divorce, at least for a time, made me feel like I had no
> idea how to make relational choices or commitments.
> This was by far the most serious relationship I'd been in.
> I'd worked so hard at it, and after fifteen years it was
> in tatters. How would I ever know whom or how to love
> in the future?
>   And since my ex-wife had an affair before our first sep-
> aration, I felt anger at her choice, and simultaneously I
> wondered why I wasn't worth being faithful to. I had so
> valued fidelity as part of our marriage. It rocked my
> world to discover such a breach. But over time, I had to

ask myself the harder questions about my own role. Greg Brown sings, "If they don't get it at home, they're gonna go looking." Had I failed to love my wife in ways that she needed?

You may also fall into both camps to a greater or lesser degree. The key is to recognize how divorce has influenced your self-esteem and to move forward consciously, to either remake it or to regain it. Robin's experience falls along both sides of the self-esteem continuum and her answer reflects the complexity of understanding what actually happens in marriage and divorce.

> Some days I feel pretty [lousy] about myself—a failure. That the marriage failed because of me ... you know ... if I hadn't "turned gay" then the marriage would have lasted. But then I remember that there were plenty of things wrong with the marriage before 1994. I had asked him to go to counseling with me long before I had any idea of this part of me.
>
> Marriage is about a sacred relationship between two people. But people change and, depending on how hard both of you work at it, that relationship can grow stronger or fall apart. The dissolution of the marriage falls on both of us.
>
> So most of the time, I like myself more now because *I* am beginning to emerge. I can say what *I* like and don't like, not to the exclusion of what others like, but also not to have myself constantly pushing down my wants and needs because of someone else or society's arbitrary judgment of who and what I am and who I choose to be with.
>
> I am a human being. I am made in the image of God, and I have value. I am stronger in this belief now that I ever was in the past—the belief that I have rights and dignity and value!

While she acknowledges the role her coming out played in the divorce, that is not the whole story. A healthy view of divorce sees both sides, as challenging as that may be for us.

Salvaging Self-Esteem

Finally, there are always people who enter into marriage with relatively low self-esteem and who hope that the marriage will strengthen their self-worth, competence, or both. Divorce in these situations deals an even more damaging blow, since they may have few inherent resources for rebuilding their self-esteem at all. Mary's story reflects this dynamic. When I asked her about her divorce and her sense of self, she could see how previous issues from her childhood combined with the divorce to create a destructive mix. The experience of her own divorce illustrates how already low self-esteem deteriorated even further during her divorce.

> My self-esteem suffered horribly. Mostly this was through thinking that I was toxic to every relationship I'd ever been in. I felt strongly that I would never be close to anyone again (not even friends) because I destroyed everything I touched. I know I felt this in some ways because of things my husband said to me, about being manipulative and holding him back from the life he thought he was meant to lead. But it went deeper than that. I was an adult survivor of childhood sexual abuse and that brings with it all kinds of sexual issues and problems. My husband was compassionate at first when he learned this, but later came to resent it and told me so. I came to believe that my damage from the abuse went all the way to my bones and this made me damaged goods and basically toxic to others. Even though I'm remarried now and in a sexually healthy relationship, this belief is one that still haunts me.

Mary's divorce brought further hurt to self-esteem already undermined by sexual abuse. Barbara's experience was similar to Mary's in that she did not feel like a very strong person prior to marriage.

> Before the divorce I felt proud to be part of a couple. I never had a high personal self-esteem but was OK with things because someone loved me. I was a responsible adult, able to run a household, a fairly good mother though some grandparents would maybe disagree. Afterward I had to constantly remind myself that I was still these things. It was hard to convince myself of that, though. Obviously I was not any of those things or my husband would not have left. I still deal with this. I haven't dated much—one man. I figure, why would anyone want to be with me? I must be flawed in many ways.

Whether you identify yourself as a regainer or a remaker, or a bit of both, you will need to address your self-esteem in the aftermath of divorce. You must take the task at hand seriously. When your marriage begins to unravel, your sense of our own value often unravels as well.

The Cul-de-Sac of the Unlovable Self

When your sense of your own worthiness is deeply damaged, you may retreat to the cul-de-sac of the unlovable self as a place to hide from the world and lick your wounds. Divorce often leads you to question your ability to love and be loved, as we heard so well from Mary, Barbara, and Jon. Jessica admitted to this temptation as well. She writes, "I feel that I was the best person I knew how to be, and I had dedicated myself to making our home and caring for his needs and was just tossed out like so much trash. It reinforced the old feelings of 'I'm not good enough to be loved.'"

Thinking of yourself as ultimately unlovable can grow from several different places. For some it is simply a reasonable response in the face of being rejected. Rejection is one of the most difficult emotional experiences for humans, especially when it comes at the hands of someone who knows you so well. Because much of your sense of value comes from belonging as one part of a couple, being rejected cuts to the quick of that sense of value and worth.

For others, claiming to be unlovable accounts for the breakdown of the marriage. It is easier to accept that you are ultimately unlovable than it is to face the choices and mistakes and decisions within your failed marriage. In an odd way it can serve as a defense mechanism, since it is a catchall phrase to explain why everything went wrong. If you posit yourself as unlovable, then you need go no further into your own self-analysis. Some even find comfort in claiming such a title for themselves, much like those who cast themselves as victims.

Like victimhood, the self-as-unlovable trap is an understandable stop on the journey. But it should function as a byway along the road, not a cul-de-sac. Ultimately, it is a paralyzing state. If you view yourself as unlovable, then you can simply give up and step out of the difficult, messy, painful, and chaotic human project of love. You also reject the design of your own creation, a profoundly mysterious process that resulted in a unique individual, one who was created for connection and interdependence with others.

Human beings as a species are designed for and worthy of love, companionship, and mutual self-giving. This is how we are made. In my own faith tradition, to claim that I am unlovable is to insult the very purpose of my creation: to love God and others. This also represents a break in my relationship with the Divine within the dynamic triad. To embrace that aspect of the dynamic triad is to face the Divine with eyes open and head raised, and acknowledge openly both my gifts and my faults. A genuine relationship with the Holy is not possible when you close yourself off to the divine power of love by claiming that you are unlovable. To maintain healthy spirituality means that you are committed to strengthening, exploring, and honoring your relationship with God. That relationship forms one facet of the dynamic triad and is the ground of your being in the world. It is also the ground of your being in relationship with others. That relationship must be based on love.

Spiritually Healthy Ways to Rebuild Self-Worth

At the beginning of this chapter, we saw how adult self-esteem comes from the intersection of competence and self-worth. What are some of the ways we can move toward a place of strength in these two areas?

Cultivating Humility

One of the hallmarks of healthy spirituality is humility. Too often our culture views humility as meekness or refers to someone who exudes humility as weak, quiet, nonaggressive (even passive), and overly willing to bow down submissively. While any one of these descriptors can fit within humility, they are not synonymous with *humility*. Humility is nothing more than radical self-honesty. I say "nothing more" with the understanding that self-honesty is one of the most difficult tasks set before you as a human being. In your humility, you acknowledge what you are capable of— both the good and the bad. It is not a focus on the bad things you have done or the belief that you are unworthy. Instead, it is recognition of the ways you have (and will) fall short of your own ideals as well as recognition of the ways you have upheld those ideals. In coming to accept both the failures and the successes of your life, you can finally move forward with clarity.

Parker Palmer, a well-known educator and writer, speaks of humility in his small but powerful book, *Let Your Life Speak*. He writes,

Years ago, someone told me that humility is central to the spiritual life. That made sense to me: I was proud to think of myself as humble! But this person did not tell me that the path to humility, for some of us, at least, goes through humiliation, where we are brought low, rendered powerless, stripped of pretenses and defenses, and left feeling fraudulent, empty, and useless—a humiliation that allows us to re-grow our lives from the ground up, from the humus of common ground.

Palmer's words strike a chord. It is hard to respond to a situation in which you have experienced humiliation with the belief that something will grow from it. But it is possible, and that is part of the journey to spiritual health.

When your self-esteem is damaged, it becomes very difficult to make an honest assessment of the things you may have done wrong as well as the things at which you have succeeded. Remember that self-esteem is primarily emotional in nature, so when it is damaged, you will walk around feeling like a bad person.

This can be exacerbated by your role in your own divorce. If you initiate the divorce, you may be plagued by feelings of guilt, pushing you to ask why you could not make the marriage work, how you could be so awful to your spouse (and/or children), and so on. If you do not initiate the divorce, feelings of rejection can lead you to believe that your entire self has been held up to scrutiny and found wanting. Psychological research shows that self-esteem is damaged whether you are the initiator or the noninitiator.

In healing self-esteem, you need to find your way toward honesty with yourself. You need to embrace humility because in humility you embrace the truth about yourself. And only by facing that truth can you move toward self-acceptance.

Tending to Your Spirit

When I ask people going through divorce what they do to rebuild themselves, the most common answer is prayer. This is the case even with those who are not part of an organized religious tradition. Prayer and meditation are mentioned time and time again as ways to calm the spirit, center the self, and bring new perspective to the situation. The spirit assumes a posture in prayer that is unlike anything else.

Over the years I have come to see it as a form of submission. For some time I hesitated to use that word since it carries negative connotations of oppression and dominance. Yet I believe that in prayer the heart is allowed to submit, or release, and by this we are liberated.

"I don't want to sound holier than thou—but I am praying more these days—before and now during [my divorce]," says Robin. "For myself, my loved ones, for others. To me, when things are beyond my control … and most things are … to let go and let God seems to be the best course of action."

Finding this opportunity for release can come through meditation as well or by exploring alternative ways of opening to the Divine. In response to a question about how she coped with the damage to self that comes with divorce, Cynthia responded:

> The support of friends, and ultimately the support of the person I am now married to. These people persisted in contradicting the negative self-talk I had become such a master of, and over time I reconnected with things that I had loved [like music], starting exercising, started taking small bits of my time for me so I could learn who I was. As I started this self-discovery, I revisited my lost Christian tradition. At that time I didn't find a connection there, but I did start exploring Buddhist thought. I realized, I guess, that even though Christian theology

didn't resonate with me, I'd opened my heart to the possibility of something greater.

Cynthia's openness to the possibility of something greater shows
how the landscape of divorce, while appearing bleak, may have
hidden springs and signs of life if we are willing to watch closely
for them.

Prayer and/or meditation can remind you of who you are in
relationship to the Divine. The divorce process has a way of
pulling you off balance by making the divorce itself the primary
focus in your life. Prayer can help to break that negative depend-
ence and reorient you. When you pray, you speak to God, who is
the ground of our being. Whether you understand this as the
powerful life force that binds the universe together or as the personal divine agent who rules over all of life, the role of prayer is
the same. You are reconnecting to the Source of Life and you are
reconfirming that you actually belong to the flow of life. Prayer
also enables you to speak to yourself, to your own heart. You
remind yourself to keep your eyes on the divine horizon and to
keep moving forward toward spiritual health. You want to be
defined by your relationship with that ground of your being, not
by another individual.

During my divorce, when I would think about my situation
and focus on my spouse, I would feel a burning hole in my chest.
But in prayer I felt a sense of release and then a sense of balance,
as if all the strands of myself had been twisted but were now
aligned, or the tumblers of a lock lined up and suddenly it
sprang open. I no longer heard the voice of my former husband,
which then influenced my feelings, actions, and thoughts, but
instead heard a reminder from God from the book of Isaiah,
"You are blessed in my eyes, and I love you" (43:4). While the
focus of your prayer or meditative life will be different, depending on your traditions and beliefs, this remains one of the best
ways to regain and rebuild your self-esteem.

Claiming Authentic Empowerment

One of the most difficult aspects of divorce is the feeling of powerlessness it engenders. This affects you regardless of whether you initiated the divorce. The process of separation and loss involves a tremendous amount of release, including giving up your cherished belief in your ability to control your own life. To regain or remake a sense of competency, you must experience a form of empowerment. What this empowerment entails will depend on your personal life situation. But this empowerment must occur through spiritually healthy self-awareness and action.

For example, during my own divorce I knew that I had the power to make my husband feel guilty. At times I even enjoyed the power my words had to shape his behavior or influence his decisions. But this quickly grew stale and left a bad taste in my mouth. I was doing spiritual damage to myself by misusing my power. I was being emotionally manipulative. I came to see that empowerment had to come from within my spiritual core and had to be about me, not about my husband. Instead of power *over* people or things, I started thinking about power *for* people or things. I found that I could influence my own environment in positive ways (by tasks as simple as cooking or gardening) and I could help to empower other people through sharing my story and helping them to reflect on their own life journeys. This also showed me that how I use my own power or influence needed to dovetail with living virtuously. The choices you make about how to live out your life in the midst of your divorce as well as into the future can enhance or diminish your sense of worth. You need to focus on making choices that align your behavior with your values and that make you feel strong and unashamed.

None of the aspects of self-esteem can stand alone if you seek spiritual health. All must reinforce and support one another. In *Let Your Life Speak* Parker Palmer ruminates about the uses and abuses of power. He notes that those who use their power in authentic ways do so when they "aim to liberate the heart." In reflecting on your own power or influence, you may wish to ask yourself questions, like these: For whom do I use my power? How can I build up my own sense of self in a way that does not tear down someone else at the same time?

Celebrating Achievement

In addition to your ability to wield influence, your accomplishments or achievements enhance your sense of competency. Divorce can be a brutal teacher because it often seems to tell you only one thing—that you are a failure. And if you are honest with yourself, you can admit that, yes, divorce does reflect a failure of your relationship and you have played a role in that failure. In my own experience, I found that while I was tempted to let the stigma of failure wreak havoc with my self-esteem, I eventually came to perceive failure in a different way—as a way of being brought back to earth, having my feet put back on the ground, and facing my own reality. At times it felt as if I had been flung to the ground and I could not rise up at all. But when I was able to stand, I could look honestly at the failure and see what it had to say. Experience is, after all, a great teacher. The failure of my marriage taught me much about myself in terms of my motives, my ability for self-deception, how I had compromised my values, and the cost of my own pride. Only by embracing that thorny and ugly failure did I come to genuine self-acceptance. As psychologist Carl Jung has said, "One does not become enlightened by imagining figures of light, but by making the darkness conscious." The embrace of failure is not meant to sound Pollyanna-ish or trivial. There are few things more difficult than looking into the face of failure and acknowledging your own role in it. But it also taught me about achievement and what accomplishments truly matter to my sense of worth and competence.

Rebuilding your life and your sense of self after divorce must include activities or actions that make you feel competent again. Whether this is competence in relationships or in simple skills, the feeling of achievement is half of the self-esteem equation. Mary found that competence came from a surprising place, a place she had not known previously.

> The other thing that helped was learning two particular skills. One was cooking and the other was painting. During my marriage, my mother-in-law had the role of family cook. She was Eastern European and a tremendous cook, preparing multiple dishes for large family dinners. My husband was the one who cooked in our house and I had accepted the role of being the noncook. But it went further than this. I was also the one who didn't just not know how to cook; I was inept in the kitchen in general. Once I was on my own and had moved, I learned how to cook (completely self-taught) and I was amazed at how it made me feel inside. It gave me some of my pride back at being able to be creative. In the other situation I took on the task of repainting one of the rooms in my house and turning it into a dining room. This transformation was slow, since I hadn't done a lot of painting previously. However, it worked and I was amazed at how self-reliant I felt. This was important to me because my husband had been the handy one around the house and I never did any kind of home improvement work. Repainting a room may seem trivial, but to my emotional health it was a pivotal activity.

Mary reminds us that what may seem trivial to others may be a boon to your own spirit. The same sense of accomplishment and competency may come from other activities, including exercise (such as starting a running regimen), job performance, returning to school, dating, writing as part of a group, spending quality time with your children, volunteering, or doing community service. While you may have to push yourself to move forward, regaining a sense of competency can bring you a surprising measure of healing.

Fostering a Sense of Belonging

Divorce forces you to think carefully about who constitutes a genuine friend or who within your family cares for you in deep, authentic ways. You learn who you can trust. Family and friends are often lost during divorce, and the pain this causes can be almost unbearable. To start the process of regaining or remaking your self-esteem, you need to surround yourself with people who genuinely accept and appreciate you. Even if it is only one such person, you must seek out that person and talk, cry, lean on, and laugh with him or her. This is the time when I recommend doing a *belonging audit*. To do this, carefully consider the groups to which you belong and the relationships that you value. As you make your way through this landscape, you will need the company of those who love you the most. Reflect on who those people are and how you can cultivate and tend those relationships.

    To rebuild self-esteem requires positive regard from others. But the positive regard must be found in spiritually healthy ways that build you up in the long run. As tempting as it may be to rush into the arms of new acquaintances who compliment you and flatter you, genuine positive regard comes from those who know you best and who build you up as an integral part of the relationship. For some, this will be found in a faith community. For example, Mallory gained strength from her church in her attempts to rebuild her self-esteem.

    I didn't dare go to a church after my divorce ... It wasn't until the pastor that I had as a teen, before my first husband, took a church in my town. I asked permission to attend the church. [He] said yes of course ... but I was so low, I thought maybe he didn't want the likes of me. This church family has been wonderful to my family. We have become active at Fellowship Church. I am the Young Women's Auxiliary leader ... I am a member of the Missions Circle. I sing in the church choir. I have been accepted by good, praying, Christian folks. Healing has taken place. I am a confident woman now.

Mallory's experience demonstrates tenacity of spirit: She was rejected by her previous church because of her divorce. For others, leaving a faith community is an important part of healing and they foster belonging elsewhere while still finding support from their faith. Jessica spoke about this.

I was not a member of a faith community at the time of the divorce [having left my childhood tradition] and I hadn't made a decision about a new faith home, although I was making some visits. So I didn't have a corporate worship outlet—although I don't think I would have attended during those first few weeks and months. I was raw and it was difficult to keep my grief concealed. I didn't want to "lose it" emotionally in public. I turned to my closest friends and family. I turned to God in a way I never had before. I was completely leveled and emotionally bankrupt and I just said, "God, I have nothing—It's up to You."

Jessica turned to her closest family and friends as well as to God for healing. While it may seem to be obvious advice, you need to remember to cultivate a sense of belonging with those closest to you. Spend quality time with them and let them carry you. This can be difficult, especially if you wish to make your own way and do not like to rely on anyone else for help. But spiritual health includes the ability to recognize when you may be weak and allow others to build you up and be your strength. Also consider how you can cultivate belonging as part of a group. Whether it is a faith community, a divorce support group, or a cooking class, finding a place to share yourself and your gifts can bring new perspective to your own self-understanding. This is one of the ways to build up your self-worth and an understanding that you have inherent value.

Connecting with Your Compassionate Mirror

As mentioned previously, your compassionate mirror is the one person (at least) to whom you can turn for honesty and unconditional acceptance. The role of the compassionate mirror is not to commiserate, but to hear your story and walk with you through the process. He or she can also help you to construct your new spiritual map. How involved you are with this person will differ for each of you, depending on your life circumstances.

The compassionate mirror is there to serve as a mentor or honored peer who points you toward a new horizon and helps you to avoid cul-de-sacs. For some, the compassionate mirror will be a person in a professional position. Jon's experience shows that once he found her, his spiritual director played a profound role in his life. He says of her,

> A superb spiritual director became for me another major healing force. I started meeting with [her] when my stress and grief were at a peak. Over two years she consistently and kindly pointed me toward hope and possibility beyond my immediate trauma. In our weekly meetings we began with silence, then talked in an honest and therapeutic manner, and she would always close with spoken prayers that made me feel that perhaps God was with me and still loved me no matter what.

Your companion on this journey may be a therapist, a spiritual director, a teacher, a pastor, a healer, a doctor, a friend, a support group, or someone else. The key is to find a person who guides you, who will speak the truth in love to you, and who accepts you.

For most of us, rebuilding or reclaiming the self will only occur with a combination of activities and experiences. The reflection questions may help you to start the process.

Questions for Reflection

1. What are some of the activities/experiences in your life that have given you the greatest sense of competence?

2. Did your divorce affect your sense of competence? If so, how?

3. Where or with whom have you felt the greatest sense of belonging? What elements created that sense?

4. How did those people/places make you feel valuable or worthy as a person?

5. When you consider your own self-esteem in the process or aftermath of your divorce, do you identify more as a regainer or as a rebuilder?

6. What are some activities or choices you might make to regain or rebuild your self-esteem?

7. What remains the greatest challenge to your self-esteem now? How do you plan to address it?

( )

Freeing Your Potential

Taking Action

The doors we open and close each day decide the lives we live.

—FLORA WHITTEMORE, AMERICAN WRITER

Spiritually healthy behavior involves making conscious choices, striving to be nonreactive, and thinking long term. It requires taking a step back and thinking carefully about how you are behaving. When you enter into the process of divorce, you may find that your behavior becomes unpredictable, surprising, even disturbing. You may find yourself crying at length or wanting to cry but being unable to. You may feel overcome by waves of anger, rage, tremendous sadness, or anxiety. Strong emotions may make you detour from your usual patterns, jumping into escapist activities such as substance abuse, spending beyond your means, or overworking. This emotional roller coaster may also prompt you to veer from rage to despondency to a strange and inauthentic euphoria. The swing of emotions can lead you to feel out of control, flailing from one day to the next. You may hide in your home for days on end or find yourself out on the town, not wanting to go home at all.

The emotional rawness of divorce, especially in the early stages, can bring you to a place of constant overreaction, manifested in the ways you speak to those around you (children, other family members) as well as how you interact with your soon-to-be-former spouse. You may be strongly tempted to flee, seeking a place of seclusion and safety. Or you may engage in tit-for-tat thinking and actions, exacting revenge for acts against you both small and large. At work you may find yourself unable to focus, feeling depressed and lacking in energy, and responding to coworkers with irritation and impatience. How the emotional tsunami of divorce affects you will depend on your life history, your perceptions of the experiences, and your personality type.

The challenge will be to find a place where you can stop and reassess how to move forward toward positive action and away from negative behaviors. As a starting point, consider recognizing that all the behaviors mentioned above are completely understandable, given the emotional power of the divorce process. Some of the behaviors in which you engage can be controlled and redirected simply by becoming more aware of them. Irritation and impatience, for example, can often be moderated when you recognize why you are feeling them and accept that they are by-products of emotional overload. You can take a deep breath, apologize for what you have said, and keep moving forward. Other behaviors, however, may require more practice and new ways of thinking. The focus of this chapter will be on examining your behaviors and exploring how they connect with your spiritual life. Then you can reimagine your actions in the post-divorce landscape.

Divorce and Unhealthy Behaviors

You should not be surprised when you find yourself making unhealthy choices or turning away from positive behavior that you know would promote your healing. We have already acknowledged how divorce tears parts of us out by the roots, and in the midst of this trauma we cope as best we can. Rarely do we get it right from the start. But looking honestly at some of the more harmful choices can assist us in naming those that are healthy alternatives and thus point us in some new directions.

Anger

One of the most prevalent emotions during divorce is anger. Expressions of anger are often the most obvious manifestation of the deep hurt you are experiencing. Unfortunately, anger can result in some of the most damaging behaviors, from the use of destructive language to physical violence. Anger clouds your judgment and adds a volatile patina to your interactions. Kate came to see that her anger was interfering with her ability to make good choices for her children:

> Divorce impacted my behavior toward my spouse the most. Initially, my anger caused me to be stubborn and very emotional in my decision making. I would purposely make choices [for my girls] that I knew would be to my benefit and not their father's. Generally, I tried to be uncooperative. After some time and after I had spent some time in small group study and a boundaries class, I learned that my poor behavior was only hurting me and, potentially, the girls.

Anger is one of the emotional responses to divorce that can benefit from specific reconstructive behaviors, which we will discuss later in the chapter.

Depression

Anger's close cousin in divorce is depression. For some individuals, the descent into depression is the result of anger turned inward. During my own divorce, I initially believed that my

depression stemmed from the tremendous anger I had toward
my spouse. I was angry at his inability to make different choices
and I was angry because I thought he should have been nobler.
(Yes, I actually used that word in my mind!) However, in the
process of therapy I came to understand that the anger I felt
toward my spouse was only part of my depression. The other
part, and the more difficult part, was acknowledging my anger
at myself. Once the floodgates of self-recrimination opened, it
was hard to close them again. I was inundated by all my choices,
words, decisions, thoughts, and actions during my marriage that
were thoughtless, cruel, and unloving. But I also started to recognize ways that I had drifted away from my spiritual center and
had lost my way morally and ethically during my marriage. I
was terribly angry with myself for believing my own lie for so
long—that my marriage had been healthy and good for me. I felt
I should have known better. All this anger at myself was manifested through depression.

For others, depression comes in the wake of rejection and
betrayal or it sneaks up on you when you see that your dreams
have died. It can also be your spirit's response to the overwhelming task of becoming a single parent, especially if you experience
financial hardship as a result. What can be surprising is coming
to learn that you may be more depressed than you realize.
Jessica speaks to this and how she became aware of how difficult the struggle had become:

> I remember having a doctor's appointment and having to
> tell the nurse what was going on—she gave me some
> names of marriage counselors and asked me if I wanted a
> prescription for an antidepressant. I said, "No, I think I
> am appropriately depressed—it's not like I am wondering
> why I feel this way." Then, about six weeks later, one of
> my clients touched my arm and said, "Is everything OK?"
> and I just lost it. I had no control over my emotions. I

couldn't eat so I had lost a lot of weight (which I didn't realize at the time) and I was going to work each day and pretending everything was normal and fine. Now I couldn't stop crying. I remember thinking—this is why people go on antidepressants! I called that day for a prescription and had to take antianxiety meds for the first month, as well as Zoloft, which had to be increased twice.

Depression can be a serious illness that affects all parts of your life. If you think you are struggling with depression, please seek medical and professional help. There are many options for treating depression and you owe it to your own spiritual, mental, and physical health to explore them.

Suicide

When the suffering of depression becomes too acute, your thoughts may slip toward suicide. Many of the individuals whom I have counseled about divorce have admitted that the thought of suicide passed through their minds at least once. For those who have not been through the divorce process, this can be very hard to understand. The process of divorce can bring pain and serious disruption to every aspect of your life because it involves your entire self. This is not simply an instance of suffering that will pass with time. It may also include personal, whole-self reconstruction, which takes tremendous time and effort. Simply put, the process is emotionally devastating as well as exhausting. On occasion, suicide may seem like the only way to make the pain stop. Jessica's comments about her own slip toward suicide illuminate the process:

I decided to kill myself. It wasn't a sad decision at all. Really. I just decided. Like you decide to go to the mall. It was just a good solution. I was physically, mentally, and emotionally exhausted. I just had to get organized and work out the details. How? When? Whether to kill my dogs, too. Yes, I would take them with me. It was the best thing for them. It's strange to think about it all again. Ultimately, it was my nieces and nephew who changed my mind. I thought—What does it say to them if I do this? That being married is everything? The only thing? That being single makes you worthless? That I didn't care about them enough to stay? That suicide is a solution? So I sucked it up and kept on slogging through it. Then God provided some very specific answers for me—I had no doubt—and I reluctantly moved forward with my life.

Jessica's poignant remark that she "reluctantly moved forward with my life" reflects just how hard life can be from day to day in this landscape of divorce. The two aspects of her life that saved her from this decision—her nephews and nieces and God—demonstrate the power of the dynamic triad in daily life. The relationships she had with God and with her extended family pulled her out of herself and propelled her forward. Though reluctant, she was able to see a new horizon in the distance.

As with depression, if you find yourself contemplating suicide, please seek medical and professional help. Despair may be one of the things you are feeling, but you cannot allow it to determine your actions.

Withdrawal

While suicide is the most drastic and permanent escape from the journey of divorce, there are other ways that we escape or hide from the task of moving forward. Mary found that she wanted to flee from the company of others. She remembers:

My divorce made me much more reclusive. I found I couldn't stand being with groups of people for very long. And it wasn't even people who were in relationships—it was just people in general. I found I wanted to be alone or with one other person. I spent the vast majority of my time alone. I stopped going to campus daily and when I did go, I went for only as long as I had to be there (to teach, or whatever) and then I'd leave and escape home ... The only time I really felt happy or strong was when I was at home, working in the garden or being with the dogs. I also spent more time walking, taking the dogs to the state park nearby, and seeing that as meditative time.

In Mary's case the time alone was probably healthy and allowed her the time and space she needed to recover and rebuild her spirit. But what about our escapist behaviors that are more harmful?

Substance Abuse

One of the most common temptations is to withdraw into the oblivion of alcohol. Kate reflects on this:

During the divorce process and after the divorce for about one year I increasingly used alcohol to cope. I had already smoked cigarettes so that continued, but the drinking escalated to a point that that is what I thought I needed to sleep at night. Again, until I spent some time in group and reevaluated the importance of being healthy for the girls, I did whatever I thought I needed.

Kate's words demonstrate that when you are in the midst of pain, you will do whatever you think you need. Because divorce is so disorienting, you may find yourself careening from one behavior to the next, seeking a safe place to land. Frances remembers her own attempt to find solid ground:

Right after the divorce I engaged in what I can see now was destructive behavior. I slept with people I did not love; I drank way too much; I just felt I was careening out of control with nothing to hold on to ... I was in therapy and dealt with that, and I don't think the floundering, out-of-control stuff lasted too long, but it was truly awful there for a while. I had quit smoking before the divorce; and then quit drinking about a year after the divorce.... My therapist challenged me. She told me she didn't think I was an alcoholic, but I did have problems with alcohol. I agreed. Quit soon after, once I took a look at all that, and went to Al-Anon, AA, for a while. That helped.

Connecting Behavior to Spirituality

The disorientation of divorce is frightening and confusing, even though it is also natural. As we reflect on the connection between behavior and spiritual health, we need to back up a bit and start at the beginning, seeing how even our most fundamental actions can connect to and reflect our spiritual lives.

One of the most important aspects of a spiritual orientation to behavior is consciously taking responsibility for your actions. This also includes the more difficult task of taking responsibility for your *reactions*. What does that look like? As a child you learn to displace responsibility for your reactions by blaming them on the actions of others. Think of the common excuse, "I only hit my sister because she hit me first!" If you find the initial action directed toward you to be egregious enough, you can usually claim that it, in turn, caused your follow-up behavior. This kind of tit-for-tat is one of the most common ways you deny responsibility for your actions

Between Action and Reaction.

I remember countless times when I felt my language and biting words to my spouse were justified because he spoke to me that way first. In essence, he had made me do it. However, wisdom tells us that the reality is something altogether different. There is a space between action and reaction. And in that space between the initial action and the follow-up reaction lies free will and choice. You choose how you respond to others and you are responsible for your reactions as well as your actions.

Here is a classic example from my own experience. The lowest day in my divorce process happened when I confronted my husband in a public space about being with his lover when he was supposed to have been meeting me. He tried to shrug it off and make light of the situation. I reacted in rage and physically pushed him while loudly calling his lover some choice names. This created, as you can imagine, a public scene. It was one of the worst, most embarrassing, most out-of-control moments of my life. Yet when I told this story to friends, they were quick to say that my behavior was justified and that my husband deserved it. They claimed, "He shouldn't have made light of the situation" or "Yeah, you were out of control, but it was only because he wasn't taking you seriously."

For a while, I let these justifications soothe me. In time, however, I realized that what I needed instead was the more subtle response of someone who could understand my behavior and why it happened, but still hold me accountable for it. The truth is that I could have chosen to react differently. I could have walked away or I could have restrained myself and kept from hitting him. Choosing to react differently would have helped me to avoid the guilt and the heartsickness I felt for weeks afterwards. But I did not choose the healthier route. Still, I remain responsible for what I *did* choose to do.

Spiritual health can be elusive until you take responsibility for what you choose to do between action and reaction. The more conscious you become of that space, the more control you will be able to exercise over your own reactions and the less others will be able to push your buttons. This is difficult because temptations abound for tit-for-tat actions. You feel the need to balance the scales and seek what is "fair." When someone does something hurtful or rude or debasing, you want to even things out. You cry out, "I'm not going to let him get away with this!" and by doing so you enter into an endless cycle, a cycle you can justify by citing the other person's initial action. This cycle is ultimately unhealthy because it allows the other person to influence or determine your actions. You no longer recognize your actions as your own responsibility or claim them as your own conscious choices.

Reclaiming the space between action and reaction helps you become more conscious about the choices you are making in terms of your own behavior. It also grants you a greater sense of control over your own life and your own heart and mind. When you do not gain this new perspective, you can get caught in a cul-de-sac of tit-for-tat, denial of responsibility, and the demonizing of your spouse. This is a particularly dangerous cul-de-sac—one you must avoid.

The Cul-de-Sac of Demonizing the Other

One of the most challenging aspects of reimagining your behavior involves how you speak about your spouse. As spiritual wisdom tells us, the words that flow from your mouth reflect the life of your heart. How do you get a handle on this? Demonizing your spouse (or a "third party," if there is one) is one of the most natural and understandable acts during a divorce. Your friends and family may even join in and encourage you in the process. Demonizing, or dehumanizing, the other means referring to the other person as evil, as fundamentally undeserving of love or any compassion or concern whatsoever. This can be done easily enough by using dehumanizing words such as *monster, animal, evil, whore,* and *crazy.* Dehumanizing others is one of the most effective ways of severing the bonds of emotional relationships or cutting the steel cord of attachment.

You may also dehumanize as a form of revenge—you are deeply wounded and strike out in response, seeking to hurt or destroy in turn. If you're the one who leaves your marriage, you may demonize your spouse as part of a strategy that makes leaving easier to bear. The same happens when your spouse leaves you; referring to your spouse as the evil betrayer allows you to cling to your sense of respectability and avoid the sour pain of humiliation. Dehumanizing the enemy is one of the key elements of successful warfare—whether national or interpersonal.

An Understandable but Unhealthy Response

There is no question that divorce brings out the worst in people. I still feel a burn of shame when I consider some of the things I said and did during my own divorce. When your emotional bonds are breaking, you may even come to hate the person you once promised always to love. This cul-de-sac is a completely understandable place in which to rest during your divorce journey. Sometimes you demonize or bad-mouth your spouse because you are deeply hurt and feel betrayed. Sometimes you do it because your spouse has done horrible things to you or your children. And sometimes you do it so you can lessen the sense of your own involvement in or responsibility for the divorce. As with the other cul-de-sacs, it is a normal part of the process (for some; not everyone hates his or her former spouse). But it cannot become your destination because it will never allow you to reach a place of spiritual health. Why not? Because if you harbor hatred in your heart, you cannot be open to the process of love toward God or others. The hatred will always obscure your vision.

I used to see this on occasion when I met someone who had been through a particularly painful divorce. One woman referred to her former husband as "The Asshole." This was true years after her divorce. Holding on to this characterization of him allowed her to do two things for herself: play down any role she had in the failure of her own marriage and protect herself against feelings of vulnerability and pain. Her emotional epithet was an effective wall behind which she could hide. Ultimately, this is a sad situation because she could not move forward into a healthy relationship. But once again we have to clarify the process here. I do not deny that her husband hurt her terribly. That is an emotional fact. Yet there comes a time when you must lift your view to a horizon that may be shaped by that pain, but is not determined by it.

This may be difficult when you admit that calling your spouse names and disparaging her may actually feel good. There is something very human in the ability to take pleasure in the debasement of another, especially when that person has hurt you. You are able to gain back some of what you feel you have lost when you verbally wound another. The sense of empowerment you feel is surprisingly potent when you verbally rage against the emotional tide of divorce and bolster yourself by calling others fundamentally *bad*. Branding your former spouse a "child" or "monster" may raise your sense of esteem temporarily because it makes him look like the guilty party. But this is the danger of a cul-de-sac. When you cannot move beyond this kind of behavior, you are effectively spinning in place. Putting down someone else to boost yourself will always yield a sense of false empowerment. All major world religions and spiritual traditions point to this reality. Genuine, lasting, and healthy empowerment comes from being loved and accepted and from loving and accepting others in turn. This does not mean that you will necessarily come to feel love toward those who have hurt you. But it does mean that the focus of your journey cannot remain on them.

The point here is not whether the names or labels are correct or not. The point is how you choose to act or speak right now and whether this can lead you out of pain to a place of spiritual health. Despite your pain and anger, you are called to acknowledge that all people, even your spouse, have inherent value as human beings. The dynamic triad points out this reality. While you yourself have a relationship with God, so does everyone else. And while you can work on, speak about, or act out of your own relationship with God, you cannot know or judge fully other people's relationship to the Divine.

This is not our role, nor do we have the kind of cosmic knowledge of others (or, more important, of God) that would allow us to judge them accurately. That is not to say that you should not call others to account—that is another matter entirely. But a life of spiritual health is difficult to forge when your own heart is completely hardened toward the value or worth of another. If you believe that all human beings are created with inherent dignity, then you must respect that dignity, even in the midst of your own pain, hate, fear, or sense of betrayal. Living a life of love-in-action is not necessarily about feeling good about that person or even liking her. Instead, it is about respecting others and refusing to act as the final judge of anyone else.

Eyes toward the Horizon

The goal of a spiritually healthy life is not to reach a particular place in which you maintain equanimity at all times, are not swayed by anyone's feeling or actions, and rarely feel anything beyond a calm serenity. Having moments of this type of existence may be possible at certain points in your life, but living day to day, this usually is not possible. Instead, you hold on to an ideal view of what you would hope for yourself and for the world: a view of your own life as balanced, free of bitterness, and truly self- and God-directed. You move toward this ideal by keeping your eyes on that horizon, but knowing you may not reach it in your lifetime. However, moving toward that horizon and keeping the ideal in view allow you to slowly transform your life as you to begin to accomplish some of the goals you set for yourself.

How do you start living this way, with your eyes focused on the horizon? Throughout this book we have pointed to the importance of constructing a spiritual map for your actions. If you consider in advance how you want to behave, you can map a direction to reach that goal. Otherwise you will constantly be pulled off course by your spouse's actions. This sounds good, but it is not always easy. For example, a spouse suddenly threatening to go for full custody of the children can threaten to capsize your ship and you may well react out of panic. But overall the goal remains the same: to set your own course of action/behavior, understand why we have committed to these actions, and then stick with them through various practices.

Controlling Your Reactions

Step 1: Developing Awareness

The first step calls for boosting awareness of your own reactions. You can practice focusing on the space between action and reaction and working to enlarge that space so you can more consciously choose your reactions. The questions at the end of this chapter are useful exercises for starting this kind of reflective process. Two additional questions to ask yourself when reviewing your past actions would be, "Why did I respond as I did?" and "How can I choose to respond differently in the future?" The key to this type of practice is learning to maintain self-awareness or self-reflection during the actual moment of conflict. For example, when you are embroiled in an argument, can you keep a "third eye" on your motives and on monitoring your reactions? Admittedly, this requires practice and means you must be willing to change your own patterns and habits. The question to ask yourself honestly is this: "Can I disengage when I need to?" Jane found this to be very difficult, in part because her spouse could be very provocative. Consider how she handled one such instance:

> My ex apparently thought that if he could provoke me into an argument that he won. He wanted to be the victim in the divorce and was very angry at me that I wouldn't play along. If he could do something to embarrass me, he would. For instance, we were having Sunday dinner with

his parents and our six-month-old son when he asked if I really thought I could deny having been frigid during our marriage. I tried to get him to see that this was a ridiculously inappropriate topic of conversation in this setting, but no way. I eventually turned it back on him, and he left the table and locked himself in the bathroom.

Jane's task became learning how to be nonreactive and maintaining a sense of calm in public situations. You will not always be successful, but simply learning to recognize the futility of engaging can be an enormous first step. David found that embracing silence and asking himself the tough questions allowed him to navigate the space between action and reaction:

During my divorce I had a very hard time controlling my thoughts and emotions, especially during the early rounds of discussion between my wife and our lawyers. The arguments about money and our son would make me very agitated quite quickly, and would lead me to unexpected fantasies about doing her (and, at times, her lover) harm. My therapist helped me a great deal to begin to control my volatility. He told me that when I had such strong feelings and impulses, I should ask myself two questions: What would I think about this action three months from now? And what would my son think of me if I actually did what I was contemplating doing? These questions were absolutely invaluable in helping to slow me down and think about the way I was reacting to my wife. I also found myself spending a great amount of time alone in silence, thinking about these questions, and the direction I wanted my life to take, especially in relation to my son. I tried to carry this silence with me, and it did help, even in the heat of future discussions and negotiations.

Step 2: Countering One Reaction with Another

A second step involves practicing your ability to counter one possible behavior or reaction with a different one. On one level, this is something I call *language substitution*. This literally means talking (out loud works best) through your answers or responses to imagined scenarios, and substituting new, healthy ways of responding. It's a great exercise to engage in with your compassionate mirror. A trusted person can toss words and phrases to you and help you learn how to respond in healthy, nondefensive ways. When I suggest this kind of approach to people who are coping with divorce, I usually get a mix of responses.

One of the most common is the admission that she does not want to work on being nonreactive because somehow she sees this as letting him "have his way." Defensiveness is always lurking just over your shoulders. "If I let him talk to me that way," she laments, "he will never stop doing it. I have to show him that I won't stand for it." As admirable as this may sound, it is a losing battle and one that will drain your spirits.

Learning to control your reactions does at least three important things for your spiritual health. First, it allows you to gain a measure of control over your own life. In this scenario, you are not responsible for your spouse's behavior. And you are not responsible for trying to show your spouse how unreasonable, hurtful, irresponsible, idiotic, unfair, mean, or outrageous she is being. Your responsibility in the scenario is to maintain your own sense of calm and control within yourself and thus tend to your own spirit. I vividly recall lamenting to a close friend about the endless back-and-forth conversations my former husband and I would have during the divorce process, discussions in which I would try to explain my perspective while wrangling with him and trying to "make him see" my point. I complained to her that I was exhausted and did not feel as if I were making any progress. She sighed and said, "You can get off this merry-go-round, you know." I was stunned as I suddenly saw the dynamic from her point of view: two people riding a carousel of blame, recrimination, and guilt, and going absolutely nowhere. It was after that shift in perspective that I started disengaging from the conversation carousel. The feeling of being in control of your own reactions and your own voice is empowering and can promote a sense of competence.

Second, you need to take seriously the amount of energy you waste when you are pulled into arguments or when you allow your buttons to be pushed by someone else. Not only are you allowing him to keep you distracted from your own journey, but you are wasting precious resources that you need in your own life and for your healthy relationships with other people.

Finally, you will feel better. Reactive, negative speech is corrosive to the heart and to the spirit. Your words can both reflect and affect what lives in your heart. The goal of spiritual health is balance and striving toward a realistic harmony. This sense of harmony is not an airy, superficial we're-all-the-same-inside attitude. Instead, it is a way of life cultivated by means of specific behaviors while consciously inhabiting the dynamic triad of self-God-others with love as a guiding principle. Robin found that with time and practice she could come close to living in this harmonious state:

> With my ex, I try not to be reactive. He still knows how to push my buttons. On the other hand ... when I don't like the track that things are taking ... I can now say it and I can walk away. I can stand up for myself calmly and rationally. I am not the best person in the world ... I am also not the worst. I try to be more patient in language and actions. In all my relationships I try to use positive, affirming language and actions.

Taking the time to learn to be nonreactive in speech is worth every minute. You must get on with the task of living and making your way through this landscape. You need your energy to help your children walk with you, for example, or simply to feed and nourish your own spirit. As silly as it may sound, role-playing is still one of the best ways to learn how to control your speech and widen that precious space between action and reaction.

You can do the same with other behaviors. For example, in my divorce process I found myself in long, drawn-out conversations/arguments with my spouse over e-mail (as well as in person). There comes a point when engaging further in these types of discussions is a moot point. Learning to recognize when that time has arrived is important, but not always easy. I vividly remember that whenever it was time to check my e-mail I would be awash in anxiety, hoping and dreading that there would be an e-mail from my husband explaining something or responding to one of my previous emotion-laden messages. I finally had to stop writing e-mails to him and literally force myself to get up out of the chair and walk outside. I started taking the dogs for long walks at the time that I would have usually been on e-mail in the mornings. The time in the woods allowed me to feel more centered and helped to give me space and perspective. Writing those emotional e-mails had become a vicious habit, one that was leading me to more suffering instead of toward greater health.

I started to examine my behaviors carefully by asking myself: What is the healthy route? I eventually came to understand my behavior as self-destructive. I learned the importance of substituting one behavior for another. In this case I could substitute walking in the woods for sitting in front of the computer.

I found that I had a host of spiritually unhealthy behaviors that I needed to replace with new activities. The most embarrassing one was that when I drove to a certain friend's house, I passed by my husband's new residence on the way. An easy detour would have added one minute to my trip and I would have avoided seeing whether his lover's car was parked in the driveway or not. But I did not add that extra minute to my trip or take the detour until a friend pointed out to me that I was behaving in a way that was self-destructive and spiritually unwise. What does an action like this have to do with my spiritual life?

The goal of the spiritual life is wholeness and peace, a balanced view of life, and an ability to engage with others with honesty and transparency. The spiritual life is also one in which my horizon is my relationship with God and how I am called to live that out in the world. When I would drive by his house, I made my dying marriage and my own pain into my horizon and led myself away from balance toward reactive self-blame and suffering. There may have come a time when I could drive by his house and feel no anxiety or pain, but I had not yet reached that point. Sometimes avoidance is one of the best strategies.

Silence can also be a good strategy, especially if it breaks you of the habit of trying to talk too much, to explain, or to overanalyze. But you must start by looking at your own actions and determining where you are moving off course from healthy behavior. For me, it also required the discerning eye of a few people who could be very honest with me and call me to account when it came to my spiritual life. These individuals became my compassionate mirrors. As I crafted my own spiritual map in response to my behaviors, I recognized that some of my goals were things that I would probably not attain within one day, one week, or even one year. Not speaking about my spouse in a disparaging manner, for example, took daily commitment, and I was not always successful. But the map made me conscious of my actions and the result was a greater sense of control and focus.

Building New Habits

When you experience a loss on the scale of divorce, you need to take the time to create new habits of the body, mind, and spirit. One of the most common among individuals going through divorce is exercise. New habits of the body (running, walking, hiking, biking) can bring tremendous relief from depression, anger, and anxiety. David, who was coping with a highly emotional divorce, shared that after he got off the phone with his spouse he would be so angry that he would fantasize at times about hurting her physically. In response, he would take his dog and walk around a local lake, walking and walking until all the anger had dissipated. This new habit, coupled with intensive therapy, allowed him to recover his spirit and move forward, in time, to a place of compassion toward his former spouse.

For David the act of walking became something that helped him to control and dissipate his anger. It became a spiritual practice. For others, exercise functions as a means of developing competence and self-esteem. It is, after all, an authentic way to care for yourself—mind, body, and spirit.

David's example may seem extreme to those who have not been through a divorce. Yet his experience is a reminder that you must take seriously the profound emotional toll that divorce can take on your soul. Wishing harm or fantasizing about doing harm to your former spouse is a reality for many people as they move through divorce.

Talk Therapy

The stress of divorce adds to the urgency of finding a compassionate mirror to guide you, to walk beside you, and to unconditionally accept you. Anger is not the problem, per se. The problem is in what you do with your anger. The number of homicides linked to divorce reveals that your deepest pain can morph into a searing rage. One of the most important habits to develop while moving through divorce is talk therapy. You may find this with a professional counselor or you may find it with a support group or friends. You may also find that it works best in combination with antidepressants or antianxiety medication. The key is to find the right person and make constructive talk a new habit. The importance of a compassionate mirror cannot be overstated.

When depression holds you hostage, finding the right person for talk therapy is critical. Depression can suck all the color, joy, energy, and meaning out of your life. It can estrange you from those closest to you, and it can make suicide look like an acceptable solution. Parker Palmer explains that "depression is the ultimate state of disconnection—it deprives one of the relatedness that is the lifeline of every living being." His own struggle with depression pushed him to engage the darkness in his own life, to search for meaning, and to find evidence of the Holy. In writing about depression, he uses the metaphor of the seasons and likens depression to the depths of winter: "Winter clears the landscape, however brutally, giving us a chance to see ourselves and each other more clearly, to see the very ground of our being." Palmer was able to move through the darkness and emerge on the other side more deeply connected to his authentic self and to God whom he sees as the Mystery of the Universe. What depression may give to those of you who go through it remains to be claimed by each one of you. Nothing is less helpful than telling someone what she needs to do in order to "get over" her depression. What is required for healing can only be answered by the one working toward recovery. But recovery is possible, good life and joy are possible, living in the light is possible—in time.

Community Service, Spiritual Practices

The role of the compassionate mirror is critical. But so, too, is the role of your friends and the nourishment you can gain by recommitting to them and fostering new habits of spending quality time with them. Engaging in community service is another habit of the heart that can foster a radical change in perspective and bring you to commit to new behaviors. Spiritual practices, such as prayer, can also confer benefits as they become new habits. Prayer, in particular, is one of the most effective ways to soften the heart and cultivate peace in your own life. For a spiritual discipline that is sure to bring transformation, consider praying for your former spouse. When I make this suggestion to people in the parish, I often get a laugh and the comment, "You mean like, 'O God, let him see the errors of his ways!'" Yet praying for those who have hurt us is one of the most powerful spiritual practices.

The Dalai Lama, in his book *The Good Heart*, reflects on a variety of Christian principles and teachings. In response to the charge from Jesus to love our enemies, he writes,

> This reminds me of a passage in a Mahayana Buddhist text known as the *Compendium of Practices* in which Shantideva asks, "If you do not practice compassion toward your enemy then toward whom can you practice it?" The implication is that even animals show love, compassion, and a feeling of empathy toward their own loved ones. As we claim to be practitioners of spirituality and a spiritual path, we should be able to do better than the animals.

The Dalai Lama is refreshingly honest about how difficult it may be to pray for your enemies, yet he is also firm in his insistence that those who call themselves spiritual people need to do this. He is a practitioner of this himself as he prays for members of the Chinese army, even though they are the ones who have inflicted the greatest damage on the Buddhist believers of Tibet.

I often think of the Dalai Lama when I am trying to dredge up compassion for those whom I call my enemies. I have found that a good start is simply saying their name while in prayer. In time, and with healing, I can usually add in more words. Prayer does have the power to change your heart. And when it is practiced alongside other new habits, you can find yourself transformed.

Two women, Frances and Robin, speak eloquently to what can happen when these new habits are put in place and we begin to move in new directions. Frances remembers,

I think I asked "Why?" for a long time (not why me, but rather, why is this happening when I have tried to do this right?) ... but finally, I got back to a life that included trying to focus more on what was right and real for me. I was a Girl Scout assistant leader in my daughter's Girl Scout troop. She and I ran together for a time—when she came to live with me after I moved out of state. I continued and continue to write. My prayer life has become more centered ... listening, trusting the answers that come, trusting myself. I try to take care of myself but I always struggle with that. But basically, I am just happier. More content. Trusting myself and trusting God without quite so many huge expectations—of myself, of life.

Frances found healing and the ability to recenter her life when she focused on her daughter and on God. Her new actions allowed her to strengthen two sides of the dynamic triad and, as we saw with Jessica, God and her daughter pulled Frances out of herself into a new life. The same was true for Robin as she came to see the centrality of relationships:

I try to be intentional about my relationships—to call and write and keep in touch with the ones I love I care about. We humans love to blame someone for our misfortunes. Well, I am not blaming God. I had a part in the end of my marriage and I think that it is fair to say that there were other people and factors involved. Instead, I turn to God in prayer. I try to make mass once or twice a week and go down and feed and eat at the homeless shelter every week or two.

I'm human—I make mistakes—but I can learn from those mistakes and do a better job of it. Like I said ... it is all about relationships ... with God, and our loved ones, and others, and creation, and ourselves.

Building a Network of Support

It can be difficult to develop new habits of thought and behavior without the help of a strong network of support. You need to be held accountable by others and you need to know that you are not alone. Those who support you can make the difference between finding healing and being caught in a cul-de-sac. By allowing them to help you, you strengthen your interpersonal bonds and you come to know more about the richness of life that awaits you in this landscape. We talked previously about the role of the compassionate mirror in helping you navigate this journey. In this section I explore some of the support you might need to develop in order to counteract the more destructive or damaging behaviors that can arise from divorce.

Support for Combating Substance Abuse

Substance abuse is one of the most common ways for people to escape from the emotions that plague them through this process, whether they are guilt, anger, sadness, frustration, or loneliness. Some are able to pull themselves from the quagmire of these habits rather easily as time goes on. Others require a hand up and out.

Alcoholics Anonymous, Narcotics Anonymous, and Al-Anon are excellent resources, and meetings can usually be found in local churches. Frances's experience (quoted earlier in the chapter) shows that these groups can offer perspective and a tremendous sense of support.

Support from a Faith Community

For others, a faith community will provide a new structure of support. While your involvement may shift following divorce, you may find a faith community that can meet your needs and bring you a sense of peace. Barbara notes:

I spent time with family and a Christian counselor. I continued to attend church and got involved with a variety of things, though not to the extent I had been before. I read the Bible a lot the first year or two. I found a lot of comfort in that and also a lot of encouragement to stay true to my beliefs.

Finding new levels of commitment can provide strength and the will to stay true to a new course of behavior or action. For Michael, this meant a return to his Christian upbringing in a very conscious way:

I began by rededicating my life to Jesus Christ. I have been a Christian since age thirteen; however, I had allowed too many compromises in my core beliefs and behaviors. I stopped drinking alcohol completely. I started listening to Christian music more, and started attending a church that better suited my level of spiritual maturity. I also changed my lifestyle to reflect less emphasis on material things, and I changed my friendships to include mostly Christian friends.

Michael also found that the practices of his tradition (study, confession) helped him to move forward. He shares:

I spent a lot of time studying divorce and relationship in the Bible and compared those to what I had learned from secular psychology. I repented a lot. I became much more humble than I had been.

Support from Family

Your family may be another consistent support network on which you can rely. Unfortunately, for some, the divorce process brings about a rupture in family relationships or demonstrates

more clearly the absence of family support. If you do have positive relationships with your family, the sense of connection can
be a source of strength. Janet found that her connection with her
siblings, which has not been particularly strong previously, took
on a new life during her divorce:

> I certainly became the matriarch of my family. My sister
> and brother became more important to me. In fact, my
> brother and I are so close now that we talk at least once
> a week and take trips together. Since we shared a similar
> experience growing up with fighting and dependency,
> and now that both parents are gone, we could feel free to
> be open with each other. I should share here that all of us
> are divorced and still single. I am the youngest and the
> leader and I am the only one at this time in a strong and
> loving relationship.

Support from Children

Your children can also keep you on the right track and help you
find joy in simple activities. As we saw with Frances earlier in
the chapter, postdivorce life can actually open up new possibilities for how to connect with your children. When your children
can be incorporated into your new habits and practices (such as
church, community service) you gain new opportunities for
even more growth and healing. And children can keep us oriented toward what is good in life. For Jessica, the thought of her
niece and nephew drew her out of her contemplation of suicide.

Support in the Workplace

While support groups, friends, family, and a faith community can
all provide a structure of support, the workplace is also a location
where networks can form, and a place where you can find surprising grace. Jon's experience demonstrates how just the right
mix of people can bring about healing in unexpected ways:

I sought out thoughtful friends and family constantly. I have no idea how many evenings I spent crying on someone's couch, or asking tough questions, or going for long contemplative walks. I also kept working, despite my precarious emotional and spiritual state. I have no idea how I made it through those years and accomplished anything, let alone being a caregiver for others. But my colleagues and friends did not give up on me. In between "serious" jobs I worked for six months doing simple graphic design in a local office. Those people loved and supported me in ways I couldn't possibly have expected from a simple part-time job. And I had just enough responsibility that it kept me from descending into complete shutdown.

In the end, all of your behaviors and actions should be congruent with your values and character, as discussed in chapter 3. For example, living virtuously means consciously choosing behaviors that reflect your values and serve to build yourself up, not tear yourself down or make you feel guilty, ashamed, or despondent. You need to hold on to your integrity during the ride on this emotional roller coaster. Your understanding of yourself as a person called by God to live a life founded on love can become your horizon. The call to this type of life is one of the few things you may know for certain when everything else seems to be in doubt. Of course, it is not always an easy task. But even being aware that it is a goal on your spiritual map can make you more conscious of it and more likely to put it into action.

Questions for Reflection

1. What are some of the negative or unhealthy behaviors that you feel came out of your marriage or divorce?

2. What are some of the positive behaviors that came out of your divorce?

3. How can you work on recognizing the space between action and reaction?

4. Has the cul-de-sac in this chapter been a temptation for you? Why or why not?

5. What are some new habits of the mind and heart you could cultivate?

6. Where/who are your support structures?

7. What are your current challenges when it comes to your own behavior?

( )

Building Bridges
of Trust

Reengaging in Relationships

In prosperity, our friends know us; in adversity, we know our friends.
—JOHN CHURTON COLLINS, ENGLISH LITERARY CRITIC

L ove is not simply a feel-good moment or a transitory experience. It is a whole-life orientation that can transform you for
the better. A life lived out of love is one characterized by mercy,
compassion, and forgiveness. Your spiritual life is nurtured
through your relationships when you spend time with others in
prayer or worship, or when you experience intimacy and pas-
sion. You can sense the greater reality of life beyond your petty
concerns—your relationships can reorient you toward whatever
has ultimate value or deepest significance in your life. Many of
the values to which you are devoted come from your spiritual
commitments. These values are, in turn, lived out within the
shifting, complex, and dynamic world of relationships. Because
of all these aspects, relationships can serve as windows into how
you know or understand God or the sacred in your life.

Love and the Web of Relationships

Family

Your primary relationship with your spouse holds deep significance and is tied to your identity and self-value. It is also the place where you discover the complexity and challenge of love. In divorce, on the other hand, you come to see where human love falls short and how it can fail. Your marriage may have been the place where your spiritual life was most obvious—in the way you felt about your commitment, in the vows you expressed at your wedding, and in your day-to-day living. You may have thought of your spouse as your soul mate and as a spiritual companion. Or you may only have hoped for these things in your marriage and not known them. Whatever the experience in your own marriage, the connection between your relationship with your spouse and your spiritual life is a profound one.

If you look outward from your spouse at the center, you can see complex networks of relationships orbiting from the most intimate (children) to the most superficial (professional colleagues, acquaintances). The same spiritual significance you associate with your idealized spouse may also hold true for your connections with your offspring. You may perceive your children as a gift from God, a sacred trust and responsibility. The complex power of love is present here as well. The care and nurturing of children requires flexible, multifaceted relationships in which you act as a moral guide for your children and connect their lives directly to your own spiritual values. You also have your family of origin—parents, siblings, and grandparents. These relationships, especially those with parents, may have served as the foundation on which you built your spiritual life. You come to know the joys and the limits of human love in your immediate family.

Further out in the relationship network, if you have a positive experience with your spouse's extended family, you may come to know or claim an entire second family and bond deeply with your in-laws.

Network of Friends

From your network of friends you gain valuable experiences of trust and companionship that can fulfill a deep part of your heart and bring you a sense of completion, meaning, and belonging. Friends connect you with the divine life through experiences of acceptance, joy, shared grief, and transformation. All your different relationships—with spouse, children, family, friends, and coworkers—offer opportunities for exploring your spiritual life as well as locations where your spiritual life is nurtured, nourished, and strengthened.

Divorce is especially painful because it rips these relationships apart, wreaking havoc on your sense of trust, belonging, and purpose. Your spiritual self may be deeply bruised, and flounder as a result.

Most of us have woven an intricate fabric of relationships over many years and this fabric is a rich brocade, thick with memory and significance. No relational fabric can remain undamaged when the tearing of divorce begins. This is because we cannot simply sever the relationships we have forged and developed since our marriage began, return to our prewedding status, and move on. Instead, we have frayed threads between families and gaping holes around children, as well as torn friendships and professional connections. We try to gather the pieces, but may find the task overwhelming. This tearing and rending has repercussions for our emotional and spiritual lives.

Ruptured Relationships

Divorce strains and breaks your relationships. Where exactly that damage occurs depends on your own circumstances, the nature and depth of your relationships, and where you place your greatest emotional investment. While not all these examples will apply to all readers, some will undoubtedly resonate for you as you look at the impact of divorce on your own relationships. How to approach and begin to heal that damage is addressed in the second half of this chapter.

Children

The deepest and most profound relationships to be affected by divorce are those with your children. This is where the destruction of divorce is seen most clearly and painfully. With few exceptions, children will suffer the most significant relational fallout from the divorce process. Research and experience confirm that divorce conjures up feelings of confusion, fear, anger, grief, and guilt in children. They may feel responsible for the end of the marriage or they may feel that they can somehow repair it. They may not understand what divorce means in practical terms and may find it difficult to think of you and your spouse as individual people with separate lives.

As a parent, you may experience crippling guilt or a pervasive sense of helplessness in the face of your children's reaction to the divorce. Some parents view the impact of divorce on their children as their failure to fulfill a sacred or spiritual task. The care and stewardship of children is often considered a God-given responsibility, and your divorce may make you feel irresponsible and even unfaithful to God. You may also feel anger or frustration when your children cannot understand the complexity of your marital relationship or when they blame you or play favorites.

Jeff's memory shows the haunting and succinct ways children can voice their primary concern when faced with divorce:

My sons were, at first, angry/hurt with the entire situation … I'll never forget the day when my wife and I met with the two of them to disclose the fact that we were separating. One son's immediate reaction was: "What will become of our family?"

The answer to this question will differ depending on your situation. But in the map-making process, there are specific, positive ways that you can address the special needs of children. This is one relationship in which the commitment to the practice of love will require the most from you. Later in the chapter we will hear from a number of parents as to how they lived out this commitment to practice love with their own children during and after divorce.

Parents

In chapter 2, Mallory noted that divorce can rupture your sense of yourself as a "good" son or daughter. She found that her divorce created a rift with her parents: They viewed her as a disappointment and a failure because her marriage broke up. For others, divorce may open up pathways to a new or redefined relationship with one or both parents. Your age at the time of divorce and your previous relationship with your parent(s) will have a role in how your divorce affects that relationship. They may offer to support you in financial or emotional ways. Or they may recoil in embarrassment and confusion or blame you for causing the marriage to fail.

Navigating these waters has its challenges because of your long and multitiered relationship with your parents. There can be tension between how they perceived you as a child and who you are now as an adult. Some parents will voice disapproval; others will be supportive. Some may express concern for your children; others may respond by cataloging the "signs" they saw that your marriage was doomed. As with all your relationships, your connection with your parents will need to be integrated into your map-making process.

In-Laws

If you were close to your in-laws during the marriage, the break and resulting separation can be terribly painful and disorienting. If, instead, you entered the divorce process with less-than-ideal relationships, you may find the breakup exacerbated by suspicion and blame. If you have children, then the complexity can grow, especially as siblings-in-law and grandparents weigh in on custody arrangements. Regardless of where the relationship stands at the onset of the divorce process, a rift usually develops. In Kate's experience, the break was prompted by blame, and the rift had repercussions for her as well as her children:

> My relationship with my mother-in-law was extremely strained during the end of our marriage. She made us aware of her opinion of where our marriage was headed and that she felt it was my fault, not her son's. She made herself available to her son and the children when it was his visitation time, but other than that, she isolated me from their family. Now we see each other sporadically and we are socially cordial.

Barbara found that her in-laws remained supportive for a time, but then the relationship changed. While at first they supported her over their own son, in time they came to accept his new wife and Barbara lost her "pride of place":

> His family was supportive of me for a while. They are totally against divorce and didn't have much to do with their son for years, wouldn't even say his lover's name for ten years. Then, at our first major joint event—high school graduation and open house—they spent some time talking with the "new" wife and decided maybe she

wasn't so bad. Then I was out and she was in. I feel now maybe they just wanted to be sure to keep the kids close by and since I had them the most, and lived down the road from them, that meant staying close with me. About that same time they began inviting only the kids to holidays and family dinners, leaving me out. Now I rarely hear from them (but, to be fair, I am not making the effort, either).

Both Kate's and Barbara's experiences speak to the changing nature of relationships with the extended families we gained when we were first married. Both also demonstrate how loyalty usually falls along expected lines, with in-laws coming to stand by their child, even if this did not happen at the start of the divorce process. Mary's case reflects this reality as well:

> At first my in-laws were supportive and loving to both of us, but that changed with time, to the point of outright rejecting and disparaging me. I don't blame them too much because it was untenable for them to be present for both of us at the same time. Plus, he needed his family. I also really didn't have much interest in staying in touch— I sent his mom letters for some time, but that eventually stopped.

All three of these women lost their relationships with their in-laws and came to accept that loss. For others, the loss of the in-law connection remains an open wound, one that may be healed in time. This was the case for Andrea:

> My family relationships didn't change, but (of course) I lost my relationships with my in-laws. I missed them horribly, but now that we're both remarried, I'm back in touch with his family.

A break with your in-laws is normal and may even be necessary. At their best, families provide support and loyalty for their own members. So, because of the shifting lines of loyalty, this can be a particularly difficult set of relationships to navigate.

Friends

As you move out from the center of your relationship network, you begin to see the impact of divorce on your connections with friends and colleagues. The effect on friendships is one that many people discuss yet few have studied in any systematic way. In a piece written for *Time* magazine in 2002, titled "Families: Who Gets Bob?" journalist Lisa McLaughlin writes:

> While there are no rules ordaining the divvying up of friends after a split, in many cases it works like an unspoken prenuptial agreement. That is, you take those friends you brought into the marriage with you when you go. You also take the friends you use more often—the ones you work with or, if you're the custodial parent, the friends with kids.

While this may sound crass, it appears to reflect reality more often than not. Your relationships with your closest friends may bend under the weight of the divorce process, but they rarely break. You may even find that those relationships become richer or deeper because of the process. Jon remembers: "Most friends were incredibly supportive of me. I don't think I lost a single significant friendship because of the divorce. And knowing what I had been through, people became even more eager to tell me their own stories, including the really hard and vulnerable parts." Many people find that their healing was supported and encouraged by their closest friends. In fact, it is often your oldest or best friend(s) who can act as your compassionate mirror. David recalled how one of his childhood friends played this key role in his own survival of the divorce process:

> I also trusted my best friend, whom I knew since ninth grade, and who lived a few hours away. He came by to see me shortly after my wife moved out, and after I had told him all of the horrible things she had done, he said to me, "I know it is horrible, but why does all of this sound so familiar to me?" He was able to get me to see that my marriage had followed a pattern of relationships with women that I had developed in high school and just kept repeating, culminating in my divorce. That was an invaluable insight, one that transformed my whole experience, as it now made me think about *myself* instead of how horribly my wife had treated me. He made me ask myself why I had chosen to spend the rest of my life with her, so that I did not repeat that pattern in the future.

Your personal friends can be your companions as you move through the landscape and they are often the best at helping you to keep on the new spiritual path you have claimed for yourself.

The place where friendship becomes difficult is in the division of mutual friends—especially couples who were "shared." Oftentimes friends feel compelled to choose sides and line up behind one or the other partner in the divorce. This may spark feelings of isolation and grief. Jolynn sums up this situation:

> The biggest change has been in my relationships with colleagues and some friends mutual to both my spouse and me. Sometimes, it has been hard to be the one not invited to events or parties or groups because the mutual friend/colleague chose to invite him instead of me. Most of my friends are married, so I sometimes feel like a third

wheel when I'm with them, and I notice that I am not invited as frequently to dinner parties and such.

The experience of being a "third wheel" and feeling left out of gatherings can be painful and isolating. How you choose to respond to these types of situations is an important component of your spiritual map-making.

Faith Community

One of the most disturbing effects on your relationships can come about within your faith community. For many divorcing couples, worshiping together was a meaningful activity within their marriage. Participation in worship services may have undergirded the spiritual significance of your marital vows or your commitment to raise children within a particular moral framework. Furthermore, years of shared work on committees or participation in social events may have given rise to complex relationships with a wide variety of people. Discussions of faith in small groups or joining with others in religious rituals help strengthen the cords between members of faith groups, resulting in networks of sacred significance. The response of a faith community to an impending divorce may range from rejection or judgment (especially in those communities with a strict stance against divorce) to warmth and loving support. The community's response may exacerbate feelings with which you are already coping, such as guilt, grief, anger, and embarrassment.

This can make for a painful mix; often believers will simply withdraw from their faith community to avoid the discomfort. The situation can become even more volatile if both partners wish to remain connected to or involved with the same faith community. Attending the same worship services as your spouse may be extraordinarily uncomfortable and painful. Exclusion from social events may lead to feelings of abandonment, and isolation may occur when once-mutual friends choose to align with your spouse against you.

Because of the close connection between a faith community and your own spiritual life, experiencing rejection or judgment from those in your house of worship can deeply impact your own trust in a loving God. You might interpret the judgment of a faith community as a judgment by God. While this dynamic is the topic for chapter 7, suffice it to say here that your relationship to God is far larger than your faith community. While it can be tempting to equate rejection by other believers with rejection by God, that is not necessarily the case. You need to see your inherent worth or value to God on its own terms, independent of the judgment of others.

Coworkers and Colleagues

Coping with divorce while trying to remain focused and present in your job can be trying. Oftentimes, your thoughts are orbiting around the situation at home while your body carries out the day-to-day activities required in your work environment. The daily emotional weight of the divorce process can bear down on you, making productivity suffer. You may also be subjected to intrusive questions, inappropriate remarks, and gossip or rumors about your personal life. How divorce impacts your professional life will depend on what type of job you hold and the circumstances surrounding the divorce. In Mary's case, her husband's lover worked in the same organization as Mary did. This prompted speculation and personal questions from colleagues. The easiest way for her to cope was through avoidance.

> It was awful. Everyone knew both of us [Mary and her husband's lover] and knew what had happened, and knew we used to be very close friends. I would go to work only for the bare minimum amount of time required of me and then I would flee home. I wanted to hide. I told

details only to my supervisor—I didn't talk to anyone else about it. I felt humiliated as it was, and I became hyper-vigilant about my privacy. Being at the same place added insult to injury because I'd see my husband driving her to work and that could throw me off for a whole day.

At work you may escape from the situation at home, or the workplace may bring it closer to you. Much depends on the relationships you had in the workplace prior to the divorce. These relationships are yet another consideration for the map-making process.

Cul-de-Sacs of Isolation and Rebound

With all the damage inflicted on your relationships through divorce, it is not surprising that you may opt for isolation instead of engagement. You may find that separating from your coworkers, family, friends, and even your children gives you the escape you need to function day to day. Relationships are emotionally costly. This is true even in the best of times, when your life is happiest. Friendships and families require emotional investment and careful tending to remain healthy and functional. Divorce can make your relationships difficult to bear. Some relationships will even come to feel like burdens.

Friends and family want explanations and they want to help you process your pain and your struggle. While well meaning, this can be exhausting. As David notes, "Other than [two close friends], I did not speak with anyone else about the divorce, as it takes so much energy to talk to anyone about it, and the fewer people involved, the better it goes, I think." Your energy is limited and sometimes disengaging completely feels like the best route.

You may also feel uncomfortable in your new, single status, and find that you make others feel the same way. Barbara realized that she had become a personal threat to other married women, a situation that has been documented for both divorced women and men:

> The thing I hated most was the "suspicion" I felt from wives. If I happened to be talking to someone's husband alone, the wife would suddenly appear on his arm. I felt like they were protecting him from this new divorcée who was on the prowl for a new husband. That was hard.

Barbara stopped attending many events, opting instead to be alone. Besides being perceived as threatening, she suddenly found that she was no longer invited to gatherings that were couple-focused, even though many of these people had been close friends of hers. This is one of the most common situations during divorce, and the feelings of exclusion and rejection it generates can push you toward isolation. As Jolynn recalled, "I have felt increasingly isolated, particularly in terms of social activities. I find that I either avoid or don't seek out social gatherings, partially because it seems awkward as a single person to be in these social situations, many of which I used to participate in as part of a couple."

Withdrawal from social situations is understandable and may be necessary for a time. Isolation becomes a cul-de-sac when you use it not as a resting place, but as a dwelling place. Isolating yourself from all relationships can keep you from moving forward into a new landscape. Your life continues to be dominated by pain and by the past. While we all heal from divorce at different rates, our reconnection with the world is a critical aspect of that healing.

A small number of people who have been through divorce will come to a place of self-imposed, partial isolation. In this case, you choose to isolate a part of yourself from the possibility of romantic relationships that might have the same depth or intensity as your marriage. This is not necessarily a cul-de-sac; it may be a place of deliberate habitation, one that is reached after a great deal of reflection, and a place in which you feel comfortable living. The isolation may be from in-depth romantic relationships or from commitment (such as marrying again).

In this kind of a situation, isolation does not extend to the rest of your relationships. We can see this in Anita's story. Her ability to trust was not just damaged by divorce; it was broken. Anita had extensive therapy and for her the decision to remain alone is one that makes her feel sad, but ultimately comfortable:

> I'm now in a relationship, but won't get married again. We've been together ten years now. As I've explained to him, I'm damaged goods, emotionally speaking. I gave so much; I'm just not capable of doing that again. I feel bad about that because he's a really good man, but I just don't have it in me. The betrayal that I still feel more than a decade later just won't let me commit again.

The cul-de-sac of isolation is an understandable stopping point on your journey and may even be a necessary one. It may be a retreat or a place of safety. You seek a harbor where you can grieve and begin coping with the depth of your loss. It becomes problematic when you remove yourself completely from the world for a long period or are unwilling to reenter life. We are made for relationship—whether that is with family, friends, or acquaintances—and we cannot be fully human or fully healed without others. The dynamic triad reminds you that your most balanced and stable life is one lived in the ever-changing nexus of relationships between yourself and others, and yourself and God. Isolation from others is isolation from love. And while your participation in love can result in pain and heartache, it remains the spiritual driving force of human life—and of human fulfillment.

The temptation to embrace isolation can come from a variety of sources—the emotional exhaustion of the divorce process, the exclusion by former friends and colleagues, or the destruction of trust and hope. Yet when you reflect on the perils of isolation, you must also be aware of its flip side—the temptation to dive into reconnection too quickly. This is the experience of "rebound." Your deepest sense of belonging may have been found in an intimate, romantic relationship with another person. However, one of the pitfalls of this new landscape is the danger of falling into a new romantic partnership too soon. This is a side effect of the profound vulnerability that comes with this process. It can also grow out of the fear of isolation.

Oftentimes, you are deeply afraid that you will never be loved again, or you find your heart aching for the love and attention that another person can provide. Your heart has been torn and you seek healing. Your ego is bruised and you want to be recognized and flattered. This is a natural aftershock of divorce. Unfortunately, your judgment may be the last thing to recover in the process because of the power of your emotional need. Jeane found this to be true in her own life after divorce:

> I was damaged from the events that occurred during my marriage. After divorcing, I entered into a "rebound" relationship with another less-than-desirable individual. Although there was no physical abuse, this person was mentally abusive, and when I finally ended the relationship, he stalked me for two years. He terrorized me any way he could—at home and at work.

Jeane was blind to the danger from this new man in her life because his flattery and attention were intoxicating. She set aside her usual good judgment and her heart took center stage. Jon found the same thing happened to him as his marriage came to an end:

> The death of love in my own marriage did make me more likely to respond to loving treatment from other people.

During the end of my marriage, I fell hard in love with a close friend, someone who was not available as a romantic partner. That was both incredibly life-giving ("My heart still works!") and incredibly difficult (there was never a chance I would get to be with her).

The key to understanding the impulse to jump into a relationship is to be honest about your own motivations and your own needs. David's experience provides a clear example of what that process of self-reflection looks like and what it can reveal:

> I was deeply drawn to [this woman] out of a desire to "fix" the brokenness in my life as soon as possible, and I found it very hard to control my feelings about her. There was a part of me that wanted to show my ex-wife that I had gotten on fine (and quickly!) without her, and there was another part of me that was a yawning chasm of loneliness, and I desperately wanted to fill that chasm. She represented joy and companionship to me, but I could tell at the time that I was frightening her with the expectations I was bringing to the relationship. But what I had to learn was to embrace that chasm of loneliness, and transform it into a realm of solitude, where I could seriously contemplate how I had arrived at this point in my life, and how I could avoid arriving at that destination again, if at all possible.

One of the biggest dangers of rebound is its ability to make you feel that you have fixed everything—and quickly! David's insight is an important one—you may be drawn to others in order to prove something to your former spouse ("See? I'm fine!"), or to prove something to yourself ("See? Someone wants me!"). This is a time to reflect carefully and honestly on your own motives and your own goals. It is also a time to embrace solitude—not isolation—a solitude that can bring insight and healing. You must not be afraid to be alone. Healthy relationships are built on love, never on fear. The difference may be hard to discern, which is why you need to step back, take a deep breath, and enlist the help of those close to you to clarify where you stand and where your heart is leading you.

The search for new connections can be life-affirming and empowering. Be mindful of what you hope to gain and consider carefully where you hope the new connections will lead.

Renegotiating Relationships in Spiritually Healthy Ways

Take the Long View

Contemporary life has accustomed us to moving quickly. We are used to rapid healing via modern medicine, rapid transit through our environment, and rapid progress to reaching our personal goals. So taking the long view when it comes to relationships can be challenging for us. However, this is one of the most important shifts in perception when it comes to healing the heart and finding your way forward. Taking the long view reorients your sense of what you can control and what you can affect within your own life. What do I mean by this?

First, taking the long view means keeping your eyes on your spiritual map and where you want to be in the future. You are mapping out new goals for yourself and it is toward those that you need to move. Part of this task will include looking closely at your relationships and deciding what you want to avoid and what you want to incorporate into your path toward healing. This can include interpersonal habits you want to avoid (such as commiseration or "trash talking" your spouse) as well as those you want to include (special time with your children, for instance). This also includes deciding who needs to know details about the process and who does not. Being conscious about choosing your relationships helps you to focus and to make deliberate choices that will aid you in your journey.

Divorce is a time of emotional chaos and vulnerability, and you can be easily sidetracked. It is easy to be distracted by fears, such as "Will I always be alone?" and "I will never find someone who loves me." These are genuine fears and they need to be respected. Acknowledge your fears, but do not allow them to skew your direction or entice you to redraw your spiritual map. If you do, you will move in circles or wander away from the spiritual path to which you have committed yourself. Taking the long view about yourself may mean chanting, "I'll be okay" or "Give it time" over and over again.

First of all, it may require asking your compassionate mirror to help you gain some perspective or praying daily for patience. These are some of the ways you will avoid the temptations of the "quick fix" or superficial responses to your deep emotional needs.

Second, it involves acknowledging that some relationships may simply be inaccessible during the divorce process. However, this does not mean that they always will be. For example, Mary could not sustain her formerly close relationship with her brother-in-law Mark during her divorce, but was able to be in touch with him several years later.

I knew that my former spouse needed the support and presence of his family, so I couldn't lean on Mark, no matter how much I wanted to—it wouldn't be fair to Mark or to my former spouse. I also had to step away from him because I knew that if we were in touch I would want to ask him about his take on things, and this would put him in the middle. It was really hard—I wondered if I would ever see him or talk to him again since I'd come to think of him as my own brother. After a couple of years passed, I found that we could communicate a bit on Facebook and via e-mail. It had to be enough—it wasn't going to be the same again, but it was something.

Some relationships take time to be reestablished. While you may need to step away from certain relationships during the divorce process (or they may step away from you), this does not mean that they cannot be rekindled in the future. This is a process of letting go and trusting that relationships built during your marriage may find ways to be rediscovered or renegotiated in the future. Not all will be salvaged, but some may be. Taking the long view about relationships also applies to those you have with your children, an issue we will consider a bit later.

Cultivate Patience

Taking the long view requires cultivating one particular spiritual discipline: patience. Obstacles will appear and you will be drawn off track. That is the nature of the process—it is one of chaos and uncertainty. But you can recommit and keep raising your eyes to the horizon. Spiritual practices can help you learn to practice patience. Spending time on focused prayer, meditation, writing, or being in nature can allow you to release your anxiety and recommit to both patience and your path.

Acknowledge Loss and Grief

You may find the loss of some relationships to be an unexpected and unpleasant surprise during your divorce, leading to confusion and a sense of abandonment or betrayal. Especially difficult may be the loss of the support and nurture you experienced in relationships with mutual friends, in-laws, or colleagues. Some of these relationships may be salvaged in time, while others will be lost permanently.

Give yourself the time and the space to grieve for what you have lost. With that grief may come anger and resentment. Your compassionate mirror can help you process some of the loss and the attendant feelings. The role of a compassionate mirror or supportive friends may be especially critical at this time, since commiseration becomes a consuming temptation. Avoid relationships built on commiseration. While it may feel good to trash those who have hurt you, it does not support or encourage your own interior health or healing. Further, research indicates that people find it very difficult to remain close friends with someone who constantly criticizes or puts down a former spouse, no matter how justified the criticism may seem. Recall the perils of the cul-de-sac of demonizing your spouse, explored in chapter 4. Focus instead on your spiritual map and where you want to go next. Cultivate those relationships that support your new path and that lead you toward an authentic, balanced self.

Lean on Those You Trust

Earlier in the chapter we looked at the concentric circles of relationships present in our lives that may be impacted by the divorce process. Coping with damaged relationships with your parents, in-laws, friends, and colleagues requires time and the answers will be different for each one of you, since your relationships are unique to you and to your life circumstances. Consider these general guidelines, which can help you move forward, when reflecting on these relationships.

Earlier I wrote about conducting a *belonging audit* to discern where and with whom you feel you belong. This includes reflecting on who accepts you and who has your best interests at heart. The belonging audit plays a role here as well. Divorce can wreak havoc with multiple parts of your life and cause suffering on emotional, spiritual, and psychological levels. You are extraordinarily vulnerable, whether you initiated the divorce or not. The nature of the process is one of stripping away, and the result is profound vulnerability. You need to surround yourself with people who can give you authentic support and love, and who will respect your vulnerability and be gentle with it. You need to be careful with whom you speak about your situation and allow yourself to lean on those who will listen and who you can trust with your heart.

Choose your companions carefully. Base your decisions on how they talk to you, how they listen, and whether you feel they have genuine empathy. Be firm but gentle with those who wish to help, but whom you do not want to include in this process. Divorce is profoundly personal, yet many people feel they have the right to know about your situation or discuss it openly with others. Guard your privacy and lean on those who hold your heart with gentleness, compassion, and without judgment.

The task of choosing appropriate support can be difficult if you have been a self-sufficient person who does not want to trou ble others. In my own case, this was the hardest task—to allow myself to be vulnerable with others when in the past I had always been the one helping them. But I learned that when it comes to healing your spirit and your heart, you cannot do it alone. Share your story with those who genuinely listen, who do not force their interpretation of events on you, and who do more than just commiserate. Lean on those who will build you up, who will give more than mere platitudes, and who will help you in following the path you are charting on your spiritual map. Trust your instincts and be conscious and unapologetic about sharing only what you want, when you want, with whom you want to share it.

Leaning on those you trust also applies to your faith or spiritual life. Leaning on God means different things to different people. The dynamic triad illustrates that your relationship with the Divine can grant you objectivity and perspective on your relationships with others, and this can be critically important to your healing. You may lean on this relationship through traditional channels of prayer and worship. But you may also pursue equally valid channels of meditation or yoga, time alone in the natural world, service in the community, or companionship with pets. These are all legitimate. You must find what sustains you. You must also discern what brings you closer to that which is larger than you are, and how you can best draw near to that which is the very ground of your being.

Cultivate Connections

Eventually, you will need to build new human relationships that can lead you into your new life and that can support you on your journey. Much of this emotional rebuilding will be done with those whom you already trust and with whom you have rapport. But for navigating a new life, you can look to new communities of practice and meaning as well. By this I mean faith communities, divorce support groups, community service organizations, and professional classes, to name just a few. These groups can give you new directions or help you fulfill old dreams. Becoming part of new social groups may not happen immediately and it may take time to find the right fit, but the task is a worthy one.

Fostering connections eases your movement forward through this landscape. New connections help you move through the losses of divorce and envision a new and positive future where you can find belonging and meaning again. They also help you to avoid the temptation of social isolation. Whether in-person or virtual, good community encourages you to grow, stretch your mind, and build up your confidence.

Focus on Your Children

If you have children affected by your divorce, your primary task will be to tend to their hearts. This task is listed last because it is of greatest importance. While leaning on those you trust and building new connections are critical, that's because they can help you be present for and engaged with your children. You must be spiritually healthy and clear about your forward progress so that you can provide a consistent and loving place for your children to dwell. The following voices address what a spiritually healthy approach to your children might look like. These are the voices of parents who have walked this path and have learned how to help their children with the task of navigating divorce in the family.

➤ *Speak to them honestly, yet with discretion.* Never use your children as a sounding board for your own acrimonious feelings about your spouse. It is crucial to avoid the cul-de-sacs of victimhood or demonizing your spouse. Despite your anger, your children need to hear your love, not lists of your spouse's shortcomings. Ellen's experience shows how you can practice speaking the truth with clarity:

> In many ways I feel closer to them [my children] and more open with them, because I'm able to talk to them more openly about the things I feel are right and wrong. I can also talk to them about different parenting styles, I can use the parenting style I prefer, and I can make my own decisions. The divorce has also forced me to find ways to talk about difficult subjects, and to make sure they understand how I feel about things. It's made me explain some more grown-up topics to them, such as how you can be divorced from someone and not love him anymore, but still care about him and/or not hate him.

Sharing some feelings with your children is appropriate. However, they are not your confidants and they are not adults. While you may be tempted to triangulate by talking to them about your former spouse, the focus needs to remain on communication done in love with the goal of fostering a healthy, balanced relationship between you and them.

➤ *Set goals for your relationship with your children and then stay the course.* Nothing is more important than consistency and open expressions of love. You must turn your attention to where we want to be with your children in the future. Your focus has to be on the child, not on countering your spouse's actions or using your child to exact revenge. This is one of the places where taking a long view is critical, as David explains:

Navigating the influence of [my son's] mother on his life turned out to be the greatest challenge in our relationship. I remember initially trying to counter everything negative that she did, which of course made life even more chaotic for my son. But then my brother told me that I had to forget this kind of reactive response, and accept the fact that I could do nothing to "solve" my son's relationship with his mother. What I had to do instead was to take a very long view of our relationship, and steer the relationship toward a goal far on the horizon, which represented where I wanted us to be in ten years. So I stopped focusing on his mother and what she was doing day to day, and focused on our relationship and where I wanted us to be in the future.

➤ *Spend time with them and listen to their concerns.* When I work with people who have gone through divorce, one of the most common regrets they express is that they did not spend enough time with their child and were not intentional about focusing on them during the divorce process. These regrets can last a lifetime and can make your journey into a new life difficult and rife with stumbling blocks.

While you believe in your heart that a divorce is ultimately inevitable and that in time the children will understand, you must not assume that your children understand it *now*. Divorce is a break that impacts children for the rest of their lives—and it is a break for which they were not responsible. As David came to realize: "Children experience the same kind of permanent brokenness as parents do, and deal with this brokenness for the rest of their lives. There is nothing we can do to heal this, but there are many things we can do to mitigate the worst effects of the brokenness."

Take seriously where they are now and listen carefully to their hearts. Spending quality time with them is important, especially if that time together includes activities that come to be special and can form new memories and forge new bonds between you. Robin was able to do this with her son and found their relationship renewed:

> My relationship with my younger son may actually be better than it was when I lived at home. He does an overnight with me at least once a week and we just focus on one another. We even took off Labor Day weekend and went to Key West. It was a trip I promised him—to go to Hemingway's House if he finished reading his summer assignment before the end of summer ... he just barely did!

Listening to their lives and concerns also means hearing them when they express their sadness, fear, and anger, and respecting where they are in their own landscape of divorce. While you want to control it and make it better, sometimes the best action is to let go. Ellen writes,

> I've had to learn to communicate with them better, to acknowledge their feelings, to let their anger and frustration wash over me instead of absorbing it. I've had to come to realize that I can't change things for them—this is part of their journey—and that's meant learning to let go. I try to respond openly and honestly whenever possible to whatever is on their mind; I try to answer their questions openly and honestly, and I try hard to make sure they know how much they are loved.

Over and over again, parents have indicated that when they enter into a conscious, focused relationship with their children, the mutual journey through divorce brings them closer. At times there is even an opening that occurs and you may find yourself in a relationship that would not have been possible otherwise. Janice's story is moving because she expresses her own journey in coming to terms with what kind of a mother she had been:

> Freed from the pressure of living in an unsatisfactory relationship with my husband, and increasingly sober, I have been able to develop much closer relationships with each of my daughters. Whereas for many years I was unsure of how I should behave as a good mother, now I think of myself as a good enough mother. My daughters actually want to spend time with me! And I enjoy spending time with the interesting young women they are becoming. Especially with my [twenty-something] daughter, I am able to talk about or hear about sensitive topics that I still cannot imagine talking to my own parents about.

➤ *Integrate your children into your spiritual life.* Whether it is through a faith community or by hiking the Appalachian Trail together, bringing your children into the sphere of the sacred in your life can strengthen the parent-child bond. It can also help to keep you humble, forgiving, compassionate, and patient within the relationship. Sharing your own spiritual practices with your children reinforces for children (and you) that the divorce is not the sum total of life. That can also help them see their value in the universe and remind them that they are not alone.

Questions for Reflection

1. What are some of the reactions or issues you have faced in your professional life or at work since your divorce?

2. Who can you trust or lean on for emotional support? What makes each one valuable in your life?

3. What frightens you the most about being on your own?

4. What are some of the ways you can cultivate connections with others?

5. What are some of your greatest concerns about your children as you move forward through this process?

6. What are your goals for your relationship with your children in the future?

7. What are some actions you can take with your children to move toward that future?

( )

Grace

The Art of Forgiveness

To forgive is to set a prisoner free and discover that the prisoner was you.

—LEWIS SMEDES, CHRISTIAN WRITER

A t a public lecture on the topic of healing, author and pastor Sara Miles was asked a question by a young audience member. "Do you believe in miracles?" After a reflective pause, Sara shared the story of a woman in her parish who had been coming to the food bank for groceries. This woman was homeless and had lost her hearing due to sustained physical abuse from her former husband. After visiting and coming to know some of the people there, she started to get involved at the food bank and began attending church. Sara went on to say that her own hopes for the woman were that she would be healed—get an education, start a new life, go on to do amazing things. This, to Sara, would have been miraculous and wonderful. However, none of these things happened. The woman continued to struggle and her life was far from Sara's vision of a renewed existence.

"However," Sara remarked, "she forgave the man who abused her." She paused and then added, "Isn't that the real miracle? Forgiveness is the real miracle."

Of all the steps we can take in the aftermath of divorce, forgiveness is the one people find the most challenging. Some would hear Sara's story above and argue that the woman's husband should never be forgiven for what he had done. And yet for the nameless woman in the story, her ability to forgive demonstrates just how far she has progressed in her own spiritual journey. Are you willing to consider forgiveness as a goal on your own horizon, too?

Before we begin, I want to acknowledge the difficulty of this subject and the defensiveness it can create within us. Of all the discussions I have had with individuals involved in divorce over the years, forgiveness is the one topic that prompts the strongest emotional reactions. Regardless of your initial reaction to the idea of forgiving your spouse, you must take a long look at this facet of the spiritual life. As you will discover, it is a central component of spiritual health and one of the best ways to manifest a life committed to loving God and others.

All major religious traditions encompass a practice of forgiving others. What constitutes forgiveness differs slightly among traditions, such as what is required for forgiveness to occur and who can be granted forgiveness. The presence of forgiveness throughout the world's faith traditions attests to its importance as part of our spiritual experience. As a spiritual practice within a specific tradition, it reaches its fullest expression in the life and teachings of Jesus of Nazareth as part of the foundation of Christianity. In the scriptures, Jesus is a figure who exemplifies the forgiving nature of God and who also teaches his followers to be forgiving, in turn. However, not all religious believers have found forgiveness to be accessible on a regular basis. Many profess to hold forgiveness as one of the highest spiritual disciplines, yet find it hard to practice in daily living. This is the reality of forgiveness. It is recognized as a spiritual discipline and a component of wisdom, yet it remains difficult to actually put into practice. This is true regardless of your faith tradition.

Forgiveness happens inside your heart. It concerns your thoughts, feelings, and behavior toward another person who hurt you, and it is limited to your relationship with that individual. You cannot forgive another person for what he did to a third party. You can only forgive him for what happened between the two of you.

Forgiveness versus Reconciliation

Do not confuse forgiveness with reconciliation. Reconciliation is a process by which the damaged relationship between two people is restored to the point that they can be at peace with each other and view each other with respect. As both parties shift their perceptions and feelings, reconciliation repairs a relationship enough for it to continue or to end in peace.

While forgiveness is necessary for authentic reconciliation to occur, forgiveness can occur without reconciliation. Some of the voices in this chapter speak about reconciliation, yet that is not the primary focus. Instead, the focus of the chapter is on granting forgiveness to others and to yourself. Asking for forgiveness is a different matter altogether. It may be part of the reconciliation process and does speak to a healthy recognition of your own role in the breakup of your marriage. However, it is often impossible to ask for forgiveness for practical reasons (distance, noncommunication, death, and so on), so I will focus here on granting forgiveness to others and to yourself. The "Questions in Asking for Forgiveness" at the end of the chapter probe this issue more deeply, in case this is something you wish to explore further.

Forgiveness and Healthy Spirituality

Why is forgiveness of others part of healthy spirituality? The ability to authentically forgive reflects the state of your heart and the orientation of your life. Spiritual health, manifested through humility and compassion, holds forgiveness at its core. Practicing forgiveness reflects an understanding about the nature of power and control and how to hold on to both. When one person forgives another, she releases her perceived right to judge and condemn the other person. This implies a loss of control over the other person as well, since holding on to the "right to judge" gives you a profound feeling of control and power. Setting it aside can result in feelings of vulnerability and weakness. Yet turning away from the desire for control or power over someone else is deeply liberating. It opens you to spiritually healthy traits, such as humility, compassion, wholeness, and joy.

Forgiveness also requires the exercise of empathy, which means the willingness and reflective capacity to enter into another person's reality in an attempt to feel and see his world from his perspective. Empathy requires practice and commitment—it can be difficult to achieve when you have been grievously hurt. Yet both releasing judgment and practicing empathy are cornerstones of wisdom: knowing and embracing your own limitations (especially over what or who you can control) and being able to see the world from another's perspective. As painful and as difficult as this is, it is vital to healing.

That said, we have to concede that forgiveness remains one of the most difficult spiritual practices. Some things are easier to forgive than others. Most of us have an unspoken hierarchy when it comes to practicing forgiveness. For example, it is easier for you to forgive those who are part of your inner circle.

You practice this in small ways every day when you forgive slights and petty hurts, recognizing that forgiveness allows you to keep moving forward in your life and work with friends, family, and colleagues. Forgiveness in these day-to-day situations keeps the bonds in your social network strong and functional. But that refers only to the daily, small trespasses you encounter.

More serious breaches of your relationships are more difficult to forgive, especially if the damage is severe or lasting.

Your ability to forgive also depends on who has committed the transgression. You hold high expectations of those closest to you in terms of how they treat you. While small transgressions committed by those close to you can be easily forgiven, larger betrayals or hurtful actions are harder to forgive because of these expectations. Put simply, you forgive little transgressions, but you expect those close to you to get the "big things" right.

In married life, your personal latitude for forgiveness is shaped by your previous life experiences, especially in other primary relationships. You discover this degree of latitude during the course of a marriage, and adjust or shift your expectations accordingly. Within most marriages, forgiveness plays a central role in settling disagreements, establishing boundaries, and sharing tasks (especially parenting). However, as marriages come apart, forgiveness usually retreats into the shadows.

How Divorce Undermines Forgiveness

Divorce disrupts your ability to forgive in several ways and for several reasons. First and most important, it ruptures your primary social unit. This is the pair-bond formed by you and your spouse that is at the very center of your daily life. This bond is the source of companionship, affection, and physical and emotional intimacy. Many of us perceive marriage to be a sacred bond, established on faith-based vows that imply permanency. Divorce is the breaking of that bond, whether it occurs through a sudden shattering or a slow disentanglement. Various betrayals and hurts may surround the end of a marriage, creating multiple fissures within the breakup.

At the heart of divorce is, ultimately, the experience and reality of rejection or exclusion. Whether you initiate the rejection, you are on the receiving end of it, or you arrive at a mutual decoupling, this is always a damaging aspect of the divorce process. You have been excluded from a private, special emotional reality, and the negative feelings tied to rejection occur whether you sparked the divorce action or not. This puts you in a defensive position with tremendous vulnerability.

When you are in the throes of this situation, forgiveness rarely figures in your reflections. When you are emotionally raw and experiencing hurt, you are unable to consider forgiveness. For some of you, divorce is the primary rupture in your life and one of the most significant emotional events. It can cut suddenly, with force and depth, or it can rub you raw over time. Either way, the wounds are usually profound. Survival is generally the first thing on your mind, not forgiveness.

Second, during the divorce process you may be on the receiving end of hurtful behavior toward you or your children. As a result, your own protection (or the protection of your children) is seen as paramount. Forgiveness is difficult to contemplate when you hold another person fully responsible for the difficult situation you are in. Related to this, you may also focus on the unfairness of the whole thing, ruminating on what you have sacrificed already for this marriage and believing the other is largely to blame for the divorce. This is a natural place in which to find yourself, as you seek to protect yourself and shield your own vulnerabilities. However, with help you can move forward out of this emotional bunker. Your perspective can become more balanced and you can consider the goal of forgiveness.

What Is Forgiveness?

To forgive another person is to give up your position of judgment against her. This means giving up the position that allows you to be the one to name the other's sin and condemn it. Forgiveness also means releasing the other person's ability to determine your actions or emotions and no longer letting him determine your behavior or thoughts. Most important, forgiveness involves developing empathy for the failures of another. This is a change in orientation that has more to do with your own internal reality than with the other person's behavior. This internal shift forms the heart of forgiveness.

For some, this change cannot occur without the other person's repentance. Your religious background or the way you were raised may have an influence on this. You must decide for yourself if you require the action of repentance in order to forgive. Does your spouse need to admit to everything he did to you that was harmful or destructive? Do you demand recognition of your position and your experience? Do you require (or hope to evoke) feelings of guilt or shame in your spouse? For some this is necessary. But you must also continually ask yourself if demanding repentance from your spouse before you will forgive him is ultimately another mechanism for control. Is this a way for you to maintain the upper hand and to hold on to your own sense of righteousness? These are questions that can challenge you as you contemplate forgiveness.

The Cul-de-Sac of Judgment and Vengeance

According to social psychology, when you are honest about your feelings of guilt and innocence, what you usually desire is justice for others and mercy for yourself. You find it easy to condemn others for their shortcomings and failures while finding justifications and reasons for mercy when it comes to your own behavior.

Jesus of Nazareth demonstrates remarkable insight into this particular human character trait when he observes in the Gospel of Matthew, chapter 7:

> Why do you see the speck in your neighbor's eye, but do not notice the log in your own eye? Or how can you say to your neighbor, "Let me take that speck out of your eye," while the log is in your own eye? You hypocrite, first take the log out of your own eye, and then you will see clearly to take the speck out of your neighbor's eye.

Jesus recognized the very human tendency to focus on the perceived shortcomings of others instead of looking honestly at your own internal life.

The reflexive desire to condemn is not the same thing as calling others to account. It is instead the belief that you have the ability to be the final judge (and perhaps executioner) of someone else. Further, this rush to judgment usually entails handing down a decision without any humility on your part or any recognition of your own role in a situation. It is done without compassion and you justify your judgments by referring to your rights, to God, or to your status as a victim. However you justify it, your judgmentalism is damaging to your spiritual health because it is usually connected with your desire for vengeance.

Biology has shown us that in the wild, vengeance is the natural companion to forgiveness. Among social creatures, such as primates and wolves, vengeance is used to rein in a member of the group who is acting in a manner that threatens the survival of the rest of the group. It is, essentially, punishment for being selfish. Vengeance can be expressed through social exclusion or physical attacks. The point is to remind the errant ones that they are part of a cooperative community; they must rely on one another to survive. Once the point has been made, the individual is forgiven and welcomed back into the clan.

In this way vengeance and forgiveness balance the social order and foster a relatively peaceful existence within the group. In human society, vengeance and forgiveness may function in similar ways when it comes to day-to-day living or everyday activities. You yell at the driver who cuts you off, but then forgive her when she ducks her head and waves an apology. This is relatively simple.

However, humans are unlike other social creatures in that we have a tendency to get caught up in a cycle of vengeance and will carry the tit-for-tat actions all the way to national and global levels. We invest ourselves heavily in the condemnation of others whom we perceive as a threat to our own interests. While this sounds like national politics, it can also be found at the personal level in the midst of divorce.

The desire for vengeance is a natural phenomenon. It occurs when you feel threatened and wounded and want to strike back. Divorce is a breeding ground for vengeful thoughts and feelings. Rabbi Perry Netter, author of *Divorce Is a Mitzvah* (Jewish Lights Publishing) notes, "If anger is a child of marriage, then anger is the midwife of divorce. Divorce is often born with anger and nursed on anger." You may judge your spouse, use words you know will hurt, or exact petty revenge for petty slights. Your deeds may escalate and you may find yourself in pitched battle whether in person or in court. Vengeance is not always murderous, but it can be terribly damaging to others and to your own soul. The more invested you become in "getting back at" your spouse, the more entrenched you become in this cul-de-sac and the more difficult it becomes to get out. Not only does the desire for vengeance sap your energy and cause you to lose your focus, but it has a way of pulling others into the dysfunction as well. Children are the most common casualties. You may speak ill of your spouse in an overt move to pull a child to "your side" or you may press for custody and visitation in ways that punish or control. Countless individuals have used their children to exact revenge. In this cul-de-sac, in particular, you can lose sight of the best interests of your children, your family, and yourself. The new and hopeful horizon is lost in the obsessive reiteration of slights, insults, and betrayals.

Vengeance is its own prison. Only in forgiveness do you come to recognize what genuine freedom looks and feels like. Exploring this will be a critical part of your journey through this landscape. Even if you are in the first stages of your map-making process and forgiveness is a goal far on the horizon, this cul-de-sac is one stopping place you must avoid from the beginning.

Revisiting Forgiveness in
Spiritually Healthy Ways

Genuine forgiveness requires a profound reorientation of your heart. It is a deeply challenging act and also a deeply spiritual one. The spiritual nature of the act is attested to by the world's major religions and is considered fundamental to your spiritual journey. When someone very close to you hurts you, that hurt can become the primary object of your attention. You become invested in the pain and the status of yourself as a wounded person. This is not to say that the pain is not real—it certainly is. But healthy spiritual life is gained by maintaining a balance between the three aspects of the dynamic triad. While you should be concerned with the nature of your relationships with others (including hurt to a relationship), that cannot be the only object of your concern or focus. Without the third side of the triad—the Divine—you face the possibility of remaining stuck in a wobbling dyad that cannot grant you the perspective you need to move forward in healthy ways. In each of the world's major religions, forgiveness is connected to the Divine, to the ground of our being. The relationship between yourself and God can allow you to shift your orientation away from a limited concern with your own pain and toward healthy spiritual life.

In Judaism, Christianity, and Islam, believers are commanded to forgive others because God forgives transgressions first. The divine nature is characterized by mercy—and this mercy must become the foundation for your own practice of mercy toward others. Jesus makes this very clear to his followers, and in Christianity the forgiveness of sin by God is the foundation of the command to forgive others. The same is true in Judaism. The Rabbis of the Talmud teach that God created *teshuvah* ("turning," a metaphor for forgiveness) even before the world was created, since human beings will, in myriad ways, turn away from God and each other. The process of *teshuvah*,

according to Rabbi David B. Thomas of Hebrew Union College—
Jewish Institute of Religion, "begins with feelings of remorse,
but involves a process or turning or actually doing something
constructive with those feelings of regret."

In Judaism, believers are expected to turn back to God
when they have fallen away, whereupon they will receive forgiveness and then be in a position to forgive others. Islam proposes
a similar position, affirming that one of the ninety-nine names
of Allah is Al-Ghafoor, the Forgiving One. And within Buddhism
you must align yourself with the Dharma that the Buddha
taught in order to free yourself from suffering. For Buddhists,
a major first step in this journey is releasing the desire to be
the ultimate judge of another person. This release of judgment
is the key component of forgiveness for all major religious
traditions.

The ability to show mercy comes from the knowledge and
experience of having received mercy within your own life. The
call to forgive others is rooted in the ability of believers to turn
to God and acknowledge their own imperfection and offense
against God or God's creation (including other people) and to
receive forgiveness in turn. The self-God side of the dynamic
triad keeps you focused on what is above and beyond you—it
calls you out of yourself and away from a sole focus on your own
life and your own pain. Just as the third leg provides the stability to a two-legged stool, so the self-God relationship gives you
the stability and groundedness to face your humanity in all its
limitations—and then to move toward forgiveness.

How Self-Forgiveness Mirrors Divine Forgiveness

The forgiveness you come to know in the divine relationship can
move you toward self-forgiveness. If you are coping with
divorce, the question of how to forgive yourself becomes of critical importance. I think about forgiveness of the self as "the

silent forgiveness," as few people talk about it and few resources are designed for it. This seems odd, when you consider how many people have raised it as an issue over the years. The struggle to forgive yourself takes place within the privacy of your heart and is not a common topic for discussion. I hope that in speaking about it here, we can come to some better understanding of what is involved and how we can move forward with forgiving ourselves.

The first question to ask is this: Why is forgiving yourself so hard? The answer is complex. The first reason for the difficulty is that regret has a very long half-life. In hindsight you have nearly perfect vision: You can see every choice, decision, and action as if under a spotlight. Being able to see everything so clearly *now* gives you the mistaken impression that you should have been able to see it as clearly *back then* too. As a result, you are certain that you could have chosen or acted differently. Perhaps you could have acted differently, but given the life experience and development you had at that point in your life, you probably could not have chosen or acted otherwise.

Another reason that it can be so hard to forgive yourself is because of how your choices hurt other people or caused ruptures in relationships. This is the case with Cynthia, who is consumed with regret for actions that affected her children during her divorce:

> The thing I struggled with the most—and still do—was the effect the divorce had on my children. I still beat myself up over it. Even though I believe they are better off, I don't know that they will ever see that—or at least they won't see it for some time.

Cynthia thought her decisions were for the best at the time, but they were not perceived that way by her children. A similar situation was shared by Frances:

I felt so guilty because of what I had done to our daughter, and I still regret that. At one point I seriously contemplated suicide, but I couldn't do that to her. Still, I think I left so much undone that I should have done. She is a wonderful, competent young woman, but I wonder what sort of person she would be today if she had not had her world shaken completely. And while I thought we were acting on her behalf, taking care of her, putting her first, we really didn't. I was too messed up and out of it at the time. And I moved away because I couldn't find a job ... but I should have stayed there with her. She lived with me once I got settled for a couple of years; I should have done a whole lot more to be there, or have her with me ... maybe I haven't yet forgiven myself for the harm I caused her. I know. I should be over it by now. She's an adult. She bears some responsibility for healing this relationship. And, in many ways, it's good. But, I still regret so much.

You might live with regret every day and you may obsess about how you could have acted differently or what the outcomes of your actions might be in the future. If your actions went against your personal values or convictions, they may lead to feelings of shame. Shame, unlike guilt, reflects the state of your whole self; you feel inherently bad. It is tied deeply with the concept of self-worth—because if you cannot accept your own behavior, you cannot accept yourself and this will affect your self-esteem. For all these reasons, forgiving yourself is challenging.

What, then, can you do? You can gain a sense of peace and self-acceptance through a variety of activities. Begin by respecting the time required for this process. As with healing other parts of your life following divorce, this work cannot be rushed. Second, be wary of hindsight. You can torture yourself by claiming that you should have known better and should have behaved differently. In the case of both Cynthia and Ellen, time allowed them to accept that they were different people in the past and they made decisions based on what they knew and felt at that time. Cynthia admits,

> It has been a slow and ongoing journey. I think I've just learned to be a little kinder toward myself. I married young and for the wrong reasons. My current marriage is strong, but it has taken a lot of work and cultivation. I know what it takes to be married now, and I did not when I was younger.

For Ellen, coming to see her decisions in a new light was the key to finding peace. She notes, "I've had to forgive myself for what I thought were the mistakes I made. I've since come to realize that they weren't mistakes—they were the only decisions I was capable of making at that time and place."

Engaging in prayer or meditation can also bring new perspective and a sense of peace. Robin finds that participation in worship helps to keep her focused on the truth, however uncomfortable:

> If my husband could have found some way to forgive me ... maybe we wouldn't be here right now ... maybe it would have been later ... maybe not at all. But that is the past and the unknown and it doesn't take into account my actions, my orientation, my desires. I am still working on self-forgiveness. There is a part in our prayers that asks for forgiveness—for what I have done, and what I have failed to do. I am sorry for my part in the failure of the marriage. That prayer at mass keeps me honest about what I've done, failed to do ... every day.

Unexpected Grace

Finally, you may come to experience grace at unexpected times or places. Jon's practice is a powerful one—to try to treat himself the same way he would act toward someone he met who was in pain. And perhaps this is ultimately what you must do: Practice being gentle and loving with yourself, as you would be for others.

> I dithered for a long time before filing divorce papers, because filing them seemed to be saying, "I am undoing the most serious promise I have ever made." I didn't think I could live with myself if I did that. But as with so many things, our places of rigidity and certainty get smoothed down by the friction of real life. And my own brittle understanding of my marriage vow (until we are parted by death) had to be revised. I realized that my wife and I truly were parted by a death: the death of love and trust between us. And I could not blame that death just on her. I was a full participant in the relationship that had crumbled.
>
> So I still have occasional moments of grief and guilt over our marriage's failure. But more often, I offer myself the same kind of grace and forgiveness that I would offer someone else: No matter what, I am still loved. And divorce is not the end of my life. I am free to breathe and to live into the future.

Ultimately, forgiving yourself is a challenge because it involves making peace with actions or events that cannot be undone. But coming to accept that you cannot change your past is part of the key to moving forward. I think of this as setting our benchmarks. Benchmarks are practices or experiences that you can use to measure your own behavior in terms of what is acceptable and what is not. In my own experience, I had to forgive myself for the public scene I made while fighting with my ex-husband, during which I physically pushed him. This act had filled me with a shame I had never known previously and raised the frightening question of how far I might go when it came to violence in an interpersonal relationship. I had never known such rage, and afterwards I felt sick for days.

Taking Responsibility

One of the ways I came to forgive myself was to accept that the action was harmful and could not be undone. I took full responsibility for my reaction and then set it as the lowest benchmark on my scale of personal behavior. I committed myself to never going there again. The commitment was not just one I made to myself inside my own mind. I sought help from my counselor and from my pastor to come to terms with my rage and to find ways to care for my spirit and rein in my emotions. I also prayed about it at length. One of the most important (and challenging) parts of the task was to admit that the behavior was wrong. I wanted to justify it, but could not. Acknowledging that I had acted very badly allowed me to repent honestly and seek forgiveness from God and from myself.

Granted, for some situations there is shared responsibility for what happened (actions carried out by both spouses that affect the children, for example), but you can still set your goals now for your behavior in the future. Clinging to the past or remaining mired in regret is not an option and will never grant you peace. It also will not free you to be fully present for those who are part of your life now. Consider your actions honestly. Be accountable and own them. Then decide where to go next. This is part of constructing your spiritual map. Look behind you and determine how you arrived here. Look forward to where you want to go in the future. Let the past serve as a signpost, directing you forward, not as a hitching post, where you remain in place. You can accept where you have fallen short and you can consciously make choices about who you will be in the future. If you are unable to forgive yourself, then you may end up in the cul-de-sac of judgment and vengeance. But the target of your skewed judgment and lack of mercy will be yourself.

Forgiving Others

Almost all the divorced or divorcing people with whom I have worked acknowledged that forgiving their spouse was something they felt was necessary in order to move forward, but they found the actual process very difficult. Those who were Christian felt the added weight of Jesus's command to forgive others and to love your enemy. Forgiveness is not to be taken lightly. It requires commitment and a reorientation of your thoughts, feelings, and behaviors. Like grief, it can be a cyclical process, one you move through again and again. This cyclical nature can be hard to face. You tend to believe that once you have been able to forgive, the situation is over and done with. This may be true for some transgressions in your relationship. But divorce is a deep and complex emotional experience. Because of the multiple levels and experiences, you may need to revisit forgiveness from time to time. Barbara found this to be quite a challenge:

> I had to forgive my in-laws. I asked them to talk to their son about his actions and I never felt as if they really tried. I had to forgive the "other woman." I had to forgive my ex. Unfortunately, this is really an ongoing process. Some days I feel as if I have done well with it; others I am reminded about everything and hate them all over again. In the eyes of many, I am really "better off," but still it is the death of a hundred dreams, not just a marriage. I will have to deal with him until death because we have kids. Every time I am reminded of another dream gone because of him, I have to forgive all over again.

Over time, with strength drawn from your network of support and spiritual habits, you may find that this cycle ends and you have truly arrived at the end of the forgiveness journey. This may take years. Your willingness to take even one step on this journey is an indication that you can regain spiritual balance in your life.

What can you expect from forgiveness? You can expect it to be difficult, but you can also expect it to be healing. Forgiveness usually brings about a change in attitude toward your spouse and toward the divorce. Kate remembers that "learning to forgive, whether it was for me or others, played a huge part in coming to terms with the divorce. It wasn't until I was able to forgive [him] and myself for our roles in the divorce that my attitude and behavior changed."

There can be a resulting change in feelings, from negative to neutral or more positive, but it will be different than the feelings you knew before. Jon picks up on this subtlety when he notes, "I had to get to a place of forgiving my ex-wife. When we got to a point of forgiving each other for our failures, it was powerful and healing. But it didn't mean that we could just go ahead with our marriage. Forgiveness felt different than bondedness."

Jon acknowledges that even though they were able to forgive each other, they could not go back to the relationship they had known previously. This may seem like an obvious statement, but it is an important point to remember. One of the false expectations of forgiveness will be that it will take away all the bad feelings and everything will go back to the way it was before. This will not happen. A fundamental breach in a relationship means things are changed permanently. However, forgiveness can bring you to a new and better understanding of what actually happened in the course of your marriage and divorce. Karin recalls how she came to a place of clarity:

I'd say I came to better understand my ex—his family background, his challenges, his worldview, what he thought he saw in me, and why we were badly matched. Likewise for myself—from the separation, divorce, and aftermath I learned about my own fears, limitations, strengths, and deepest desires, what I got out of the marriage and why I needed to move on in the way I did.

How Forgiveness Works

How does the process of forgiveness actually work? In many ways it is mysterious. A combination of factors moves you to a change in perspective over time. This change in perspective is seen as "reframing" the situation—you come to view the person, the action, or the situation in a new light and with a more open heart. Empathy and compassion come to the fore while anger and judgment retreat. Jared's description of his own shift is quite dramatic. Sometimes the shift can come in one moment:

> I definitely had to work on forgiving my ex-wife. I felt betrayed by her. It is a process that I know is still going on in me. I sometimes still have pointlessly negative feelings toward her, and when I become aware of them I try to deconstruct the impulse and let go of it.
>
> The first discrete moment that I can remember of letting go of bitterness was about two months after my wife came out to me. I was alone on the beach—pacing back in forth in front of the ocean, cursing my bad luck. I became aware of the ocean—its vastness and age, as well as its "impersonality"—and my insignificance next to it. For a moment I was able to step outside myself and see that I was a very small thing compared to the rest of the ocean of being. The experience had the effect of making my hurt feelings feel insignificant.
>
> I have tried to maintain that perspective. I often fail, but I continue to strive toward that larger consciousness.

For others, the change comes over time with an accumulation of factors, such as a change in lifestyle or circumstance, time in therapy, religious reflection, and so on. Mary found that an accumulation of events shifted her perspective, although one moment in particular granted her a key piece of the forgiveness puzzle—empathy with her former spouse:

> I had moved to a new city and so I was away from being reminded of him and I had also been through some excellent therapy. I thought I had come to forgive him already, but it was a story I heard one night that pushed me completely into a new place. At a book group at church, I heard a woman describe the end of her marriage, although in her situation she was acting exactly as my husband had in my marriage. Since I like this woman a lot, I found that hearing it from her actually helped me to understand my husband's position better. I didn't want to understand his position because he was, after all, rejecting me, but I found I did understand ... and the forgiveness became more real.

Eventually, Mary also empathized with the third party in her divorce, although this required more time:

> The forgiveness of my husband's lover took a bit longer, since she had been one of my closest friends. But I also recognized myself in her (when I was really honest with myself) and I knew—to my own shame—that I would have probably acted in the same way she did if I had been in the same position. I guess I understood her weakness because it was familiar to me. Years later she asked for my forgiveness (once he had left her as well), and it was good to realize that I had already forgiven her.

All these voices show that empathy, humility, and compassion are critical for the process of forgiveness. How have people gained this level of spiritual insight? Joining a support group, talking with a compassionate mirror, and reading spiritually oriented books were all named as effective starting places by people I have counseled. These resources can help you change your thinking and they can also facilitate a shift in feelings.

One of the most effective means, however, for moving yourself forward is prayer or meditation. In my own practice, I draw on images from a powerful story about the Buddha's life. In combating anger and hatred toward his enemies, the Buddha would meditate at length. In his meditative imagery he would see lines of soldiers facing him with arrows drawn. When the arrows were released, they flew toward him in the air, but before reaching him they morphed into flower petals and fell harmlessly to the earth. This image helped me to stay true to the direction I had set in my own spiritual map. The Buddha's actions highlight an important dynamic of forgiveness. The soldiers (or your spouse) may still have arrows. The arrows may still be aimed at you and they may still be released in your direction. The change is in how you perceive the arrows and the soldiers. The Buddha strove to love the soldiers by recognizing their common humanity and by turning their hatred away with compassion. He demonstrates that the key to transformation lies within your own heart and mind. It is here that you must focus your efforts, not toward changing the other person. And while I cannot boast of having his skill at meditation, I do know that directed meditation can transform the heart if done regularly and with a skilled teacher. Prayer can also bring the same kind of healing over time, especially if you commit to the practice of praying for your spouse.

Both prayer and meditation can become cornerstones of the final test of forgiveness—your behavior. When you have fully forgiven your spouse, you no longer seek to hurt him, you refuse to rise to provocation, and you have a sense of disconnection that is healthy and empowering. The flame of vengeance dies and turns to ash. Your focus becomes something completely new—an open vista whose view is no longer blocked by your own anger, fear, or despair. You may well feel some residual sadness. Grief for the "death of a hundred dreams" may always stay with you. But your life has new direction and new hope.

In time, you may finally be able to say with Frances, "I have discovered that forgiveness is everything. Forgive ... again and again and again. It is the only way to freedom."

Questions in Asking for Forgiveness

All theistic religious traditions teach followers to repent after committing a violation against God or one of God's creatures. Your decision to ask another person for forgiveness is laudable if it is done solely for the purpose of seeking peace for yourself or reconciliation and/or closure. Here are some questions to use in the process of discerning whether asking for forgiveness is appropriate at this point in your journey.

1. Clearly articulate the reasons why you wish to ask someone for forgiveness. Why forgiveness for this? Why now?

2. Are you seeking closure for yourself or have you been focusing on the desired reaction of the other person?

3. In asking for forgiveness, can you be content with making your request, even if the reaction of the other person is negative or hostile?

4. Can you disengage yourself emotionally and spiritually, if the reaction to your request for forgiveness is one of hostility?

Questions for Reflection

1. Has forgiveness played a role in your spiritual life? If so, how?

2. How did you experience forgiveness within your marriage? Did you ever discuss it explicitly with your spouse?

3. In terms of your divorce, is there anything for which you feel you must forgive yourself? Why might this process of forgiveness be difficult?

4. Looking at your divorce today, would you say there are actions for which you wish to forgive your spouse? If so, what are they?

5. What are your own challenges in terms of shifting your thoughts, feelings, or behaviors toward forgiveness?

6. What do you think the benefits of forgiveness might be for your own spiritual life?

7. How does forgiveness play a role in your relationship with God or the Divine?

( )

Know Thyself

Coming Closer to God through the Transition of Divorce

What we are is God's gift to us. What we become is our gift to God.

ELEANOR POWELL, AMERICAN ACTRESS

A fundamental premise of this book is that, because we are spiritual creatures, we must be attuned to the spiritual reality of life. That spiritual reality affects how successfully we navigate the landscape of divorce. At the apex of this reality is your relationship with the Divine. How you understand this connection to the sacred impacts all other aspects of your life. This means that relationships and behaviors become holy if your relationship to the Divine is the ground of your day-to-day living. It also means that your connection to the Divine can influence how you perceive others and how you act on those perceptions.

This is especially true of marriage and family because, for most of us, these are sacramental in nature and are the place in which we live out a spiritually oriented life. Also, marriage is a ritual that usually takes place within a spiritual setting with profoundly binding language. Couples come to see their marital union as a sanctified relationship—a union blessed by God and set apart from all other relationships. When you perceive the Holy in your life, even the most mundane activities (dinner with your children or walking in the woods with your spouse) can become imbued with a sense of the sacred.

Spirituality is a reality for a majority of Americans, but how this is lived out differs among faith communities and individuals. Marriage and family are almost always a significant part of your spiritual understanding of life, regardless of your faith tradition. Divorce strikes this sense of the sacred at its very core and can turn your spiritual orientation into chaos and confusion. How divorce affects this part of your life often depends on how much conscious reflection you have done regarding your own relationship with God. Have your assumptions or beliefs been challenged previously? Do you still believe the way you did when you were young? Have you explored your spiritual life or asked probing questions? How multidimensional is your faith and your spirituality? How flexible is it? The resiliency of your spiritual life may depend on the answers to some of these questions. Research has consistently shown that those with more flexibility in their belief system can weather the traumas of life more easily. Not only can you stand strong in the face of challenge, but trauma can actually spur growth within your spiritual life.

The spiritual dissonance of divorce may impact your relationship with God in a number of ways. Let's look first at how divorce can instigate struggles in the way you understand or think about God. Then we will consider how divorce can lead to struggles in how we think about ourselves *in relationship with God*. These two perspectives may overlap and become mutually reinforcing. Ultimately, for a healthy spirituality to develop, these struggles must be taken seriously, examined, and resolved.

Struggling with God

Struggles in your relationship with God may show up as dissonance in your concept or understanding of who God is or how
the Divine works in your life. For example, you may have been
raised to believe that being a good person (living honestly, going
to services, not lying or stealing, and the like) granted you protection from bad things happening to you. This may never have
been an explicit lesson, but it was still an expectation that is
challenged when you are confronted with pain or when things
do not go according to plan. In the face of divorce, you cry, "But
I did nothing wrong! I've been a good person! How can this happen to me?"

The Exchange Model

This struggle reflects a relationship with the Divine based on
exchange. In this view, you will live your life according to the
will of God, and God will protect you in return. When confronted with the reality of your divorce, you will ask, "How could
God do this to me?," a question that may be fueled by anger and
a sense of betrayal. Your relationship with God was supposed to
be a shield to protect you from the slings and arrows of life. This
was the case for Barbara, who prayed for her marriage when she
learned of her husband's infidelity.

> I grew up in a very conservative Baptist home. Divorce
> was wrong except in extreme circumstances. I believed
> God wanted us to stay married until death. And, because
> I knew this to be God's will, I couldn't believe that He
> would not answer my "prayer according to [God's] will."
> I had always been taught that God answers every prayer
> with "yes," "no," or "wait" and that [the Divine] always
> answers according to [God's] will. Well, [God] didn't.
> While I still believe God *can* do anything, I now see that

[the Divine] doesn't always do *something*. Way too many
people tell me God is in control. Well, I am having some
problems with this concept in that things did not go
according to what the Bible says [God's] will is.

Barbara came to question the idea that God was always in control because she prayed for God's "will to be done" within her
marriage, and yet it did not happen. Barbara had always
believed in God's control of the world. But she did not count on
her husband's choices and the fact that God appeared to allow
his choices, even though they contradicted God's will. She
found that her concept of God was conflicting with her lived
experience.

A similar situation happened with Jeremy. He thought he
knew what was required of him by God, but found that his life
experience did not fit that view. In this case the struggle happened directly with his spouse and ended up affecting his relationship with God. Jeremy's wife wanted a divorce, against his
wishes. They were both Christian and had been raised to believe
that divorce was a sin against God. For Jeremy, the separation
and divorce pushed him to reevaluate his beliefs.

It did nudge me toward reevaluating why I believed in
God, if Christian people like my spouse are not even willing or able to follow some of the basic teachings of
Christianity, like loving your spouse and children, and
putting them (especially children) ahead of yourself. I
guess the Christian God doesn't really have much effect
on how—some, many, most—people live their lives.

For Jeremy, the spiritual struggle with his wife eventually led
him to agnosticism. They each held very different perspectives
on God, and this prompted a break in his relationship with God.
The plan of how to make a God-centered marriage work had

failed. This made Jeremy question God's role in any of it. Robin, on the other hand, found she had sympathy for this position, but ultimately came to see the struggle in a different light.

> People often have bad things happen in their lives and they shake their fists at heaven and say, "Why, God?" I don't particularly feel that bad things are the work of God. God has given us the ability to think, to reason, to choose right from wrong. Most of the ills of society are of our own making. But I do acknowledge that there are some things that happen that are beyond my understanding and I'll just have to live with that ... for now.

Robin's ability to accept that some things are beyond her understanding enabled her to come to terms with her divorce. She took the initial step of working to discern what she was responsible for in the situation, and then moved forward using the gifts of reason and judgment that God had given her. This also allowed Robin to take some responsibility for what had happened within her marriage—a critical step for spiritual health.

Jessica needed the same type of reflection and discernment to come to terms with her situation. For Jessica, being married was part of God's plan for her life—this was something she had come to believe very deeply. Her understanding of God included the idea that God lays out the plan and we follow it. She could not comprehend how God would allow her to experience divorce when it so clearly contradicted God's plan for her.

> I was [ticked off] at God. Really. Then that eased and I just forgot about God for a while because it was too painful. I think that was easier than thinking the divorce was part of God's plan. I don't believe God has a plan—in the sense that everything in someone's life is predestined. That just doesn't make sense to me. If that were so, you

could jump off buildings and survive because "It just wasn't your time." I had a lot of questions about God that I don't think I even allowed to fully form in my mind during that time.

For a while, her anger at God shut down Jessica's spiritual life completely. In time she would come up with a new way of thinking about God or being in relationship with God—but it would require releasing old ways of thinking and considering new possibilities.

Related to this struggle with the idea of God's plan or will is the question of how you come to discern what God's will is for you *after* your divorce. For example, in my own experience, I believed that marrying my husband was what God wanted me to do; my marriage was part of God's plan for my life—or so I thought at the time. This was a powerful experience and it gave me a sense of certainty in my marriage and a firm belief in the spiritual purpose underlying it.

When the marriage ended, however, I was forced to rethink what I had believed about where God was calling me, and I had to reexamine my own ability to discern what the purpose of my life was. I questioned my own judgment when it came to spiritual matters and I wondered, how would I even know or recognize a new path for myself? How could I figure out where God wanted me to go if I got it so wrong previously? I had been traveling a particular road and it was one filled with possibility and dreams. Suddenly the road ended. There was no warning (or there was and I ignored it) and I had to exit. This experience was profoundly disorienting and placed a burden on my relationship with God. My question became, "O God, where do I go now?" This situation, like that of Jessica above, had to be met with some new ways of understanding God's work in my life.

Your struggle with the Divine may parallel what you saw with Barbara and Jessica, or my own situation. For others, that struggle will take shape in a different way. Jeff's experience speaks to those who have enjoyed a consistent and mature relationship with God that now has been lost. This struggle focuses not on God's will or plan, but on the presence of God in your life. Jeff was employed in a faith-based organization and had extensive theological training. To outsiders he appeared to be a person in touch with the Divine and someone who could function as a spiritual model. Following his divorce, Jeff lost his sense of the presence of God: "I have had a hard time centering. I have a hard time praying. I wrestle with this sense of loss of direction. I *want* God, but I can't seem to find my way toward God."

While this sounds like the loss of a plan or direction, the reality goes deeper. Jeff no longer even knows where to start.

> I think God loves me. I know God is there, but I just don't know how to approach God at this point in my life. I have a deep longing for a meaningful relationship with God but I don't know the terms for that any more; I've lost the vocabulary; I feel linguistically challenged when it comes to communicating with God these days.

For someone who always had the words to speak of or to God, this has been spiritually debilitating. Jeff finds himself wondering these days, "Where is God in all this?" This type of struggle within your relationship with God is not surprising, given the emotional and spiritual toll of divorce.

Finally, a shift in thinking may take you to a deeper place, a place of new insights into God and yourself. David's Jewish upbringing taught him about the sacred nature of marriage, and that this view reflected what God wanted for God's people. His divorce pushed him to a different concept of God:

> I came to see that one person cannot keep a marriage going. Even if one person believes that God intended

marriage to be an inviolate bond, that doesn't mean that the other person will believe it or hold to it. It becomes intolerable—then you're trying to hold someone there who doesn't want to be there. God was with me when I let her go. My view of God shifted from the one who is a guarantor of human commitments to the One who is with us in our brokenness. And that view has stayed with me.

Struggling within Ourselves

Divorce may lead you to ask not only about God's relationship to you, but also about your faithfulness to God in return. For example, during and after divorce, you may feel disappointment or guilt that you have not lived up to the expectations you feel God had for you. This is especially true when the marriage ceremony took place in a religious setting and was understood as a sacred act. Guilt develops if you believe that God called you to a particular way of life and you failed in that calling. This can be the case whether you are the initiator of the divorce or not, and can be made even worse by the presence of children.

It may be difficult for those outside of a faith community to understand the depth and power of guilt in response to divorce and how this can fray your connection to God. For those raised in faith traditions that explicitly prohibit divorce, this experience of guilt can be devastating. You struggle with the voice in your heart that whispers, "You didn't try hard enough" or "You made those promises to God; you have to sacrifice for them" or "You're a failure in God's eyes" or "God gave you those children—now look what you're doing to them."

In more intense cases, this might lead you to believe that God has completely rejected you because of your failure to live up to the vows you made. This experience of guilt can be compounded by your faith community if the faith group considers divorce to be a personal spiritual failing that places you outside the bounds of community. Some people even experience overt rejection by clergy or other religious leaders, as Frances found in her experience: "I felt abandoned by the church and friends that had known both of us. I remember going to churches and ministers not knowing what to do or say to me and ignoring me ... I would sit there and cry. So, that didn't last long. I just quit going for the rest of the time I lived in the same town." The rejection by a faith community may have lasting repercussions and may result in an all-consuming, personal experience of shame and rejection. As we will see later, for some people a relationship with God continues, but they become wary of its expression within a spiritual community. You need to come to terms with guilt and resolve this spiritual struggle in order to make the journey back to wholeness with God and to explore the possibility of forgiveness.

All these ways of struggling with God—your understanding of the Divine, your beliefs in a divine plan, your sense of your own faithfulness—can combine and overlap to create severe disorientation and emotional pain. All along, you have believed that life is generally good, that God is with you, and that your life is the product of your own choices and behaviors. You believe that you reap what you sow on a cosmic level. Your life and your marriage have been good and you feel grateful and blessed. Into this rosy view of life comes the ax blade of divorce.

Suddenly, you are thrown back in confusion and no longer know what to believe about life in general. People you love betray you, those you trusted try to destroy you, and you are threatened with losing everything that is most precious to you. Nothing is certain anymore. The doubts and fears reach down to the bedrock of your assumptions about the goodness of life and the decency of other human beings. It also calls into question your understanding of how God works in the world and who is ultimately in control of your life. This can lead to existential anxiety and a top-to-bottom questioning about "what the point is" of anything you do. However, this disorientation may also set the stage for you to understand the deepest and most profound truths about human existence. Nothing is certain in life. All things are fleeting. This breakdown of your worldview may create space for an expanded relationship with the Holy, allowing for a new, more complex understanding of the Divine's nature.

You can come to see that your life has meaning and purpose because you can effect change and make life joyful for others. Reaching this state of wisdom means that you are finally able to look at the reality of human life in all its brokenness and yet commit to a life of love and compassion *in spite of* this reality.

The Cul-de-Sac of Despair

Because the tension in your relationship with God can manifest itself in different places and within different relationships, the cul-de-sac associated with God is a complex one. The overarching term is *despair*, which reflects a loss of hope. A loss of hope may be seen in a number of ways, but here we will focus on three that speak to the human-God relationship: bitterness, shame, and rejection.

Bitterness

Bitterness is an interesting emotional state because it can be expressed in a variety of ways. For instance, in a more overt expression, a bitter person exclaims, "God owes me. I did things right and this is what I get?" This form of bitterness grows from the exchange view of relationship. Akin to banging on a vending machine that has eaten your dollar without giving you your snack, you shake a fist at God and lament about getting a raw deal. In a more inward-focused bitterness, you may become wrapped up in the question, "What's the point?" and slide into a place of existential emptiness. I have done everything right, so the thinking goes, and I still end up on the losing end of things, so what's the point of even trying?

Both these examples arise from a similar place—the idea that you are owed protection. This orientation, while understandable in the divorce process, is ultimately simplistic. This becomes a cul-de-sac when you refuse to consider the possibility that God works or functions in any other way. For your own spiritual health, you need to consider the possibility that God is infinitely more complex and mysterious than you previously assumed and that faith is more than just earning protection from suffering. We will see a bit later how some people's vision of God expanded and led them out of this cul-de-sac.

Shame

In the second iteration of this cul-de-sac, you find the focus more on yourself and on your own spiritual life and struggles. The most common place of entrapment here is related to guilt and how it can morph into shame. Guilt is a social emotion that arises when you violate your own values or the values of someone you respect or to whom you are committed. Shame, on the other hand, reflects the wrongness of your entire self. It is the difference between "I have done a bad thing" (guilt) and "I am a bad person" (shame). When you are burdened with guilt, it can morph into shame, and this can be debilitating. If you feel you have failed God, it can be very difficult to regain a sense of yourself as valuable, loved, and forgiven. This experience of shame can overlap with the divine struggle when you come to believe that not only are you guilty beyond redemption, but God has abandoned you because of your transgressions. What makes this a cul-de-sac is the potential for becoming trapped in guilt and shame and sensing no possible redemption for yourself.

There is much to be said for those who can practice radical self-honesty and admit to their own responsibility for the failure of their marriage. Being able to take responsibility for your actions is, after all, the hallmark of spiritual maturity and health. However, when you become beholden to guilt or shame, you end up spinning in a slow circle, feeling worse and worse, and more and more useless. This kind of intrapersonal struggle can become a cul-de-sac when you are no longer able to carry out your day-to-day duties. That is, you can no longer see yourself objectively, you cannot complete your work or tend to your responsibilities at home or on the job, and you are unable to relate effectively with others or with God. In the final section, we will hear about how it is possible to step out of the cul-de-sac of guilt with the help of others.

Rejection

Finally, your spiritual struggle with others may result in the complete rejection of any type of faith community, especially if your faith community has judged or rejected you. Your rejection of community may become a cul-de-sac if you stubbornly refuse to engage with others or close yourself off to the possibility that communion with people seeking spiritual expression will result in anything positive. This can mutate into derision toward faith communities or a sarcastic attitude toward "organized religion." Without a doubt, a certain critical distance from community can be a very healthy thing, and for many people the path toward spiritual health involves only a tangential relationship with a community of believers. The cul-de-sac is formed when the perspective moves from "healthy critical distance" to "completely off-limits." Not only does this stance close you off to the potential for spiritual community, but it can also close you off to God.

All three of these positions within the cul-de-sac are examples of despair because they lack one thing: hope. You have no hope of receiving anything new or different from God, no hope that your guilt could be lifted or your shame redeemed, and no hope that you can find a spiritual community or home. All three are also completely understandable and may be valid aspects of your journey. As with other cul-de-sacs, the problem arises when a resting area becomes a dwelling place. When that happens, you are moving away from spiritual health, and your connection with the Divine will suffer. Each of these positions represents an imbalance; in each, the self has become disproportionate. In essence, you have lost perspective on yourself.

I gained insight into this cul-de-sac a few years ago when I heard the life story of one of my students. Angela was born into wealth and privilege. She had the best of everything until her parents divorced when she was thirteen. The divorce was particularly brutal and she, her older sister, and her mother ended up homeless. They moved from shelter to shelter and Angela fought to remain in school. During that first year after the divorce, she often did not have enough to eat and her bitterness grew until it was evident in her speech, her mood, and her interactions. She was angry all the time. Bitterness had replaced gratitude. One moment she had everything, and then she had nothing. Her anger at the unfairness of it all was a constant companion. This all changed in a moment, when after a particularly challenging day she was complaining bitterly to her sister about their plight. Her sister looked at her and said, "What, you think you're the only person who has lost everything?" Angela explained to me that from that point on, she saw the world in a different way.

Suddenly, she could see other people and what they had lost, and she saw herself as just one among millions of people who had lost, and gained, and lost again. She had a radical change in perspective—a turn toward empathy. Her perspective shifted from a focus on her own plight to actually seeing the plight of others—and in this shift in perspective she found hope. She lived out her hope, in high school and later in college, by becoming an advocate for those who had no one: the homeless, migrant workers, battered women. While her own problems still plagued her, her focus had shifted. Instead of living in despair, she chose to live in solidarity. This allowed her to be a source of hope in the world.

Angela's story serves as a reminder to me: While grief and moments of despair are real, they are not the only reality. You can be of no use to others and cannot be a source of light in the world if you are consumed by your own darkness. In each of the cul-de-sacs, we see the dynamic triad out of balance. The self has grown disproportionately large and is pushing out the Divine, as well as other people. Simply put, there is no longer room for God, for gratitude, or for hope. If you acknowledge that this is understandable and the pain of the self is real, how then do you move back to a place of balance? In the following section we will see and hear how men and women going through divorce have avoided or moved out of the cul-de-sac of despair and found new ways to think about and connect to the gifts of the divinely inspired life.

Renewing a Relationship with God in Spiritually Healthy Ways

You can renew or reestablish a relationship with the Divine in a wide variety of ways. Here we will consider three of these ways: turning toward community, embracing spiritual practices, and pursuing intentional reflection.

Turning toward Community

One of the most reliable ways of renewing your relationship with the Divine is by being part of a faith-based community of like-minded people. This might be a traditional house of worship, but it might also be a support group or service organization. Community can be very powerful and may bring us experiences that provide comfort, insight, and growth. However, community can also be a place of pain and rejection. For those going through divorce, sometimes community is viewed with suspicion, as the church may have been a place of judgment. Frances maintained her relationship with God, but there was a break with her faith community and she felt wary about renewing a relationship with that community after her divorce:

Even then, my understanding of God was separate from what I thought about the church. God was there ... with me ... forgiving ... I just floundered for a long time, but did not feel God was absent. I did not feel judged by God ... I felt judged by the church, but I kept trying to figure out what God wanted me to do.

For Frances this meant searching for a community that would not judge her—a task that took courage and perseverance. Frances's story exemplifies how it is possible to move out of a cul-de-sac of rejecting community. She found that she had to take a break from traditional sources of shared spirituality, as the judgment she had experienced cut to the quick. This is the case for many people who go through divorce. As it turns out, the group of people most likely to leave their religious community permanently are those who have gone through divorce. This is a telling statement about how traditional forms of shared spirituality have failed those whose marriage has broken up. Yet Frances never closed the door on the possibility of finding a loving, supportive group again. In time, she did. She knew that her relationship with God was not complete without a spiritual community of some kind.

Marriage may have kept you in a faith community that was not your home. Divorce then may grant you the freedom to finally find your true spiritual home. In Ellen's case, the divorce allowed her to search for a community in which she could express her unique brand of spirituality, one that had always been within her:

I joined the Unitarian Universalist Church late in life [age forty-seven], but I have always considered myself very spiritual. I find a great deal of connectedness with the universe and the world around me while outdoors, watching animals and birds, or experiencing the seasons

firsthand. I pray every day, and I give thanks on a regular basis for my blessings and gifts. I believe very
strongly in the power of prayer. I also love the ritual of
my church—the music, the sermons, the celebration of
community—and I enjoy serving as a worship assistant
and volunteering around my church for the sense
of greater good and feeling connected to my fellow
parishioners.

Like Ellen, some find that divorce grants them the freedom to
pursue community and explore a part of themselves in a new
context. Jeane found that once she was free from the confines of
her marriage, she could seek out a community where she could
come to know God:

> While I was married, I wanted to pursue a spiritual path
> by seeking out another denomination [non-Catholic] in
> which to raise my son, and worship together as a family.
> Although my former husband never went to church, he
> refused to even consider visiting a church that was not
> Catholic. His statement was "We are Catholic." I could
> not understand why he took such a rigid stand on being
> "Catholic" when he didn't even go to church. After my
> divorce, I was finally free to pursue other church options
> and found a wonderful [non-Catholic] church where my
> son attended Sunday school and made his Confirmation.
> So I would say my divorce allowed me to finally have a
> relationship with God.

For some, the task of finding a community may mean going
back to what you knew as a child from which your marriage had
separated you. For Janet, it meant returning to her Catholic
roots and finding that, "Going to confession and mass regularly
was like salve on my wounds." In the midst of healthy commu-

nity, you become free to worship, share, talk about, or explore ideas, and find a connection with the Holy. Robin's return to a worshiping community led her to experience the Holy through traditional Christian means:

> I do believe that there is value and need for communal gathering and sharing and affirmation of faith. So there I go for Sunday and Holy Day services. Sometimes in communal song I feel that tingle of the Presence. Sometimes it happens in the breaking of the bread and the lifting of the cup. Sometimes it is in the private prayer in the time after Communion. In the sacraments, prayer, and song, there is a synergistic energy that makes the whole spiritual experience so intense and powers me up to go out and serve others, as is the call of my faith.

Sometimes your engagement with community will not come through traditional means. Nontraditional forms of spiritual community can be more powerful, for some, than traditional means. Janice had experienced rejection from her church, but found a place in Alcoholics Anonymous. AA can be a profoundly spiritual community, a place where many find their way back to life in relationship with the Divine. Janice notes,

> I never thought I would hear myself say this, but through my involvement with Alcoholics Anonymous, I have learned the benefits of developing an attitude of gratefulness. I try to make it a practice to thank God for the good things (usually small, seemingly coincidental events) that I notice in my daily living. Similarly, I am learning to look at the proverbial glass half full, instead of complaining about all the things that are lacking in my current existence.

The importance of community is found not as much in its *form*, as in what it provides in terms of *content* to those who gather. If it provides a place for deep, spiritual self-reflection that allows you to ask questions about the meaning and purpose of life, then it helps to move you toward spiritual growth. If it allows explorations of who God is and what being in relationship with God might look like, then it leads you toward spiritual health and wholeness.

Embracing Spiritual Practices

One of the most important benefits of connecting with a spiritual community is the place it provides you to practice your spirituality. The role of spiritual practices cannot be overstated: They are an essential aspect of the spiritual life. The goal of spiritual practices is to reestablish balance in the dynamic triad as well as to strengthen the bonds within it.

Practices are habits of mind, heart, or body that bring you a connection to something that is larger than yourself. Examples include participating in worship, prayer, or meditation; reading spiritual texts; engaging in fellowship, discussion, and retreats; fasting; offering hospitality; and doing service work. Practices are about the alignment of the heart and mind. They should bring you back to balance, but also make you open to the movement of the Divine within your life and in the world. Daniel Homan and Lonni Collins Pratt, authors of *Radical Hospitality,* hold that a spiritual practice "is an action intended to make a change or adjustment in the deepest realm of the self. A spiritual practice is a thing we do that opens a door." Homan and Pratt seek to share the power of spiritual practices to bring about transformation in your life and in the life of a community. If you are going through the process of divorce, these spiritual practices can help keep you balanced and focused on the horizon while helping to strengthen or restore your relationship with God.

What makes a practice spiritual is its intentionality. How you enter into a practice is important: Do you affirm its ability to affect you in powerful ways? Do you see it as a way to connect with God? Michael's experience shows how his practices evolved out of his background, and how they shifted over time:

> I express my spiritual life first by educating myself about *where* and *how* a spiritual life can be achieved or developed. Since I was raised with a traditional Protestant background, I have been taught to read the Bible, pray on a regular basis, seek fellowship with like-minded Christians, and serve others in a way that would honor God. How I achieve these goals is varied and has changed over time. At my age now, I spend less time reading the Bible and spend more time reflecting on what I have read. I pray with less asking and more seeking and waiting. I experience God more in people, the arts, and nature than I have in the past

Like many divorced individuals with whom I have worked, Michael found that losing his marriage changed his approach to God. The shift was toward more listening, especially in prayer. This shift toward listening is one I hear about often. It reflects a more humble approach to God, an openness that indicates a willingness to hear new things or see aspects of life in a new light. Prayer with an emphasis on listening is a "thing we do that opens a door," mentioned by Homan and Pratt, cited earlier. This open-door policy is one that often emerges from divorce, reflecting humility and a willingness to learn about the spiritual life from new sources. Robin engaged in spiritual discussion with others as a practice that allowed her to grow and that opened a door within her as well. In this case, it was through participation in an online course:

I took online classes ... on Catholic Social Teachings. We had discussion boards and on them I was able to read and converse with a deacon who was a Cuban exile; a lay brother doing missionary work in Nicaragua; a Catholic lesbian in Maryland; and all sorts of parish, diocesan, and regular people of faith. One of the most powerful witnesses of faith in those classes was a homeless woman who took her classes diligently from a computer in the public library. Despite her situation, she spoke convincingly of a loving God—merciful, forgiving, and enduring. She gave me much to consider and reflect on.

The practice of fellowship and discussion allows for new insights and new learning. It is also one of the best ways to challenge your own perspectives or views about God, the spiritual life, and yourself. This shifting of perspective can come about through a combination of practices. Jolynn's practices include reading, conversation, and silence:

I express my own spiritual life on several levels in several different contexts. On a personal, individual level, I practice prayer and meditation daily, read books on topics relating to spirituality and religion (mostly the former), and I seek out others for conversation on spiritual topics. I also go on a silent retreat at least once a year for five days, when I meet with a guide for several minutes twice a day and otherwise allow the time and space for thoughts, feelings, images, or whatever, to emerge. My community involvement in spirituality includes both regular attendance and participation in a local congregation and participation in smaller groups with no particular religious affiliation. These smaller groups meet to discuss spiritual topics, share experiences, learn spiritual practices, and explore various ways to navigate the spiritual path (including Sufi, Buddhist, Christian, Jewish, and other belief systems).

Jolynn's many practices raise an important point—the role of silence and solitude. Not all your spiritual practices will take place within community. Often your times of retreat and solitude offer the greatest potential for finding balance, keeping yourself and your own worries in perspective, and meeting God.

I found this to be true in my own experience during my divorce. While my time with a gathered community was important, it was my time alone in the woods with my dogs that proved to be essential. Walking my dogs to the foot of a nearby waterfall several times a week became a spiritual practice for me. I intentionally opened my mind and heart and tried to let the physical motion of walking become a prayer of sorts. Naturally, this was not always easy, because I was often flooded with anxiety and worries about my life—what I would do next, where I would end up after my divorce, and so on. However, the point of practices is to allow room for the Holy to move within you and to get out of your own way. Sometimes this works best in silence. I found that standing at the foot of the falls made me feel very small and made my problems seem insignificant in comparison to the millennia that nature required to form the gorge in which I stood. At these moments I understood the biblical character of Job when God spoke to him out of the cloud, saying, "Where were you when I laid the foundation of the earth?" (Job 38:4a) The majesty of creation allowed me to shrink in comparison—a shrinking that was surprisingly liberating. I always felt more in balance when I was reminded that the Creator was the foundation of my dynamic triad.

The key to effective practices is not whether they are carried out within a traditional religious setting. The key is intentionality—whether you enter into them with open eyes and if you are fully conscious of what you hope to gain. That is no guarantee that you will always find what you are searching for. In fact, you may be surprised. My walk to the falls did not begin as a spiritual practice, but morphed into one over time. The walking became a place to converse with God, even in silence.

While Jolynn's practices were multidimensional, some simpler practices are just as effective when trying to forge a connection with the Divine. This is what Janice discovered. Her practice evolved out of her conservative Christian upbringing and helped her to move forward in her spiritual life to a new place:

> My meditation practice seems to revolve around taking note of which hymns and gospel songs are on my mind, and consciously singing them with a new, more progressive interpretation of the messages about salvation and God's grace than what I understood in my childhood.

Janice found that focusing on music could bring her closer to God. The same thing may happen with other artistic pursuits. Creative endeavors often serve as excellent spiritual practices, since they allow you to engage different parts of your mind; can shut down the nagging voice of anxiety or worry; and can confer on you surprising peace and groundedness. Openness to God may occur when your hands are otherwise engaged. Consider what some of these might be for you while you are on this journey. I have known men and women who take up painting, write poetry, work with clay or beads, engage in dance or music—all are possible ways to experience the sacred within your life.

A final note about incorporating spiritual practices into your life: In previous chapters I noted the need for patience when it comes to recovering from divorce and finding a new path through this unfamiliar landscape. The same plea for patience holds true here. Jeff's earlier question—"Where is God in all this?"—is one that can only be answered in time. While Jeff found that he lacked the language to approach God, he could still approach the Holy in silence. Jeff's situation reveals that, as with any genuine, authentic relationship, your connection with the Holy will ebb and flow. Your engagement in practices is one way to maintain the connection and to make sense of the changes that occur over time. The key is persistence and patience. Faith does not, after all, act like a spiritual vending machine, as much as we might like it to. I do not insert prayers and expect healing to pop out. Faith is an ongoing relationship; it is also a shifting, dynamic reality that changes over time. The task is to hold fast to the relationship and seek the nuances and messages, even if those come in the form of the still, small voice within.

The point of practices is to bring you to a place of balance and congruence. They also strengthen bonds between you and others and between you and the Holy. Ideally, spiritual practices should bring you insight that leads to humility. As Michael remarked succinctly, "I have become closer to God because of my divorce. By reading, praying, and talking about my divorce to others I see that I am just as self-centered and weak as everyone else, and I need God in my life to help me make wiser choices and to honor him with my life."

Pursuing Intentional Reflection

Michael came to see the truth about himself as a result of his spiritual practices, most of which were done within the context of a community. What he gained from his practices was a greater sense of his own weakness, which led, in turn, to being able to be in relationship with God in new, fully honest ways. The place Michael came to was one of humility.

Humility is a key component of a healthy spiritual life. Earlier we focused on how humility underlies truth-telling and radical honesty. Coming to see yourself truthfully, with all the bad and the good, may be difficult. Divorce is one of the few

experiences that strips people down to the core. If you are willing to be conscious and reflective during that stripping away,
you may gain beautiful new insights into who God is and who
you are called to be in the world.

Understanding humility usually requires intentional reflection. Turning toward community and embracing practices are
excellent ways of reconnecting with God or coming to a more
complex, mature understanding of the Divine. However, it is the
process of reflection that allows you to gain the benefits of these
actions. In reflecting on your experiences—whether alone, in a
group, or with your compassionate mirror—take a step back
from the immediate involvement in the activity and pause to ask
yourself, Why am I doing this? What is challenging here and
why? Where is God in this? Reflection is required to detect and
understand the motives for your behaviors, and it is one of the
best ways to focus your awareness so that you are living consciously and proactively instead of sleepwalking through life,
reactive and unaware.

One of the primary emphases of this book is the importance
of reflection. Thinking about your thinking and thinking about
your feelings are crucial if you hope to keep moving forward on
your path. Some of this can be done with your compassionate
mirror. Some can be done through journaling or prayer. Some
can be done in support groups or in classes. However you
choose to do it, you must make the time to engage in reflection
and push yourself to ask important spiritual questions. Both the
Buddha and Jesus posed questions to their followers, constantly
pushing them to reflect and diligently search for answers to spiritual questions. When you take the time and find the place for
this type of reflection, your mind and heart mature, open up,
and come into alignment with the universe.

Perhaps the most poignant example of this comes from
reflecting on the nature of your own failure within your marriage. Earlier in the book we met Mallory, who was consumed

with guilt for initiating her divorce and moving her children away from their father. Mallory's situation was compounded when her parents and her church community condemned her actions, even though she felt she was protecting her children. Mallory moved over a thousand miles from her previous home and started her life over again. But she could not join a new church because she was consumed with guilt and was convinced that God would not forgive her. Mallory was stuck in a cul-de-sac, and it was only when a new minister reached out to her that she came to see how she had been going around and around in circles. After participating in the new faith community and reflecting a great deal on her situation (especially through the practice of writing) she came to see the error of her ways: "I thought that perhaps God couldn't forgive me for getting a divorce. I was wrong. Who am I to say my sin is too big for God to forgive? I'm not *that* great ... but [God] is."

Mallory came to see that by thinking of herself as unforgivable, she had elevated her status, making herself disproportionately important in the grand scheme of things. She admitted that this perspective constituted a form of spiritual arrogance, viewing herself as more significant in the cosmic scheme than she actually was.

What Mallory has taught me is that while your guilt may be real, if you seek spiritual health you must be willing to accept forgiveness and then move on. This is a critical requirement of spiritual health—not only the willingness to forgive, but the willingness to accept forgiveness for your own actions. This also points to the potential power of confession and repentance. In some faith traditions, these are sacramental rites. Even in traditions where this is not the case, participation in confession and acts of repentance may be life-giving and remarkably liberating. Janice's reflection on her own spiritual journey allowed her to admit, "I have developed a greater appreciation of God's grace and forgiveness ... a fuller sense of how I am one of God's creatures, created by God and not such a hopeless screwup, as I thought for many years."

The process of asking questions and engaging in reflection can lead to new insights about God that, in turn, enable you to develop a more holistic, fulfilling spiritual life. This process and the end result of reflection were very clear in Janet's story. Her intentional reflection brought her to a new place in her spiritual life:

> My questions have led me to pull away from radical Christians, who tend to believe that it's their way or no way. My God is not so rigid. My God is all-inclusive and forgiving. And certainly not so judgmental. My relationship with God includes giving thanks for everything given to us, including our planet and all the voiceless creatures that count on us for their survival ...

Coming to a new understanding of God allows you to develop a new relationship with the Divine as well. This can happen when the pain of divorce is transformed through reflection to provide new answers and new insights. Jon's insight was very important in the process of moving forward after his divorce:

> I have become more and more convinced that God is a lover who pursues us unconditionally, whose love does not fail, as human love always can. I think I mistakenly equated human marriage with divine blessing. When my marriage failed, I felt as if God had rescinded a gift God had previously given to us. So now I have a much looser and more mysterious understanding of God's providence, God's involvement in our lives. I am hesitant to assign to God any particular blessing or any loss. Instead, I focus on God's loving and healing presence being with us through everything that our lives and our choices may bring.

Jon's ability to release his previous views of God allowed him to enter a new phase of his spiritual life, one bolstered by a greater sense of mystery and a new focus on love above all else.

When you engage in reflection, you are on the path to wisdom. You are responsible for your relationship with the Divine. This means that you must ask your own questions and seek your own answers to the deep questions of your life. The divorce process, painful as it is, makes room for this to happen.

Questions for Reflection

1. What are some of the ways that your divorce has caused you to question or think differently about God?

2. Have you seen the effects of bitterness, guilt, or rejection of others in your own experience?

3. What role might spiritual community have in your healing process?

4. What are some spiritual practices in which you can engage that might deepen your relationship with God?

5. Why are these particular spiritual practices valuable to you?

6. What are some of the ways you have engaged in intentional reflection during your divorce process?

7. Have you had any new insights about God, or has your spiritual take on things changed? If so, how?

8. Did any of the voices shared in this chapter speak to you in particular? If so, which one(s), and why?

9. How would you describe your relationship with God now?

( )

Moving Forward

Growing into the Next Phase of Life

Don't ask what the world needs. Ask what makes you come alive, and go do it. Because what the world needs is people who have come alive.

—HOWARD THURMAN, AMERICAN WRITER

Throughout this book I have reiterated the importance of creating a spiritual map for yourself so that you can actively craft your future as you move through and out of the divorce process. The map that you carry in your head and heart reminds you where you want to go and who you want to be in the future. It reinforces where you do not want to end up as well—in the cul-de-sacs of victimhood, feeling unworthy of love, demonizing your former spouse, isolation, or despair. Instead, you can venture toward a horizon of spiritual health buoyed by humility, strength, responsibility, empathy, forgiveness, and wisdom.

A life of authenticity marked by honest self-reflection will help you avoid the temptations of reactive and self-justifying behavior. The reasons for spiritual map-making are twofold: (1) the positive benefits that spirituality can provide for coping with trauma and (2) the knowledge that approaching problems proactively and consciously can bring about desirable ends.

Contemporary psychologists of religion have long seen the positive connection between spirituality and coping with traumatic life events. Many religions teach the importance of deriving spiritual truths from the experience of suffering. A strong spiritual life will not protect you from suffering, but it can help you transform suffering into growth, insight, and wisdom. It can connect you to what is greater than yourself. Robin's description of the spiritual life spotlights how spirituality can permeate all aspects of your life:

> I think that spiritual people believe that there is something greater than themselves in the world. That life is more than the sum of cells lumped together and put into motion by electrical impulses. That there is meaning and purpose in our existence—not just a "poor player who struts and frets his way across the stage and then is heard no more ..." to borrow a line from Shakespeare.
>
> But it is not enough to just "believe" abstractly—spiritual people consider their whole life in relation to this belief. It may affect their actions, their associations, and how they live their life. For me, I guess, spirituality is all about connectedness. It is something inside of me and outside of me and is about all of us.

Robin's spirituality is grounded in connections between herself and others and herself and God. These connections are the heart of most people's lives, and a healthy spiritual life will permeate all of them. Because spirituality is not a protective device, traumas that you experience may lead, in turn, to spiritual struggles. According to psychologist Kenneth Pargament in his *The Psychology of Religion and Coping*, these spiritual struggles usually show up in three areas: the Divine, the intrapersonal, and the interpersonal. These three areas parallel the nodes of the dynamic triad. When you go through a trauma of some kind (such as the death of a loved one, a divorce, a job loss), you may find yourself struggling with questions about God, feelings about yourself, and issues involving relationships with others. This book has focused on those struggles in relation to divorce. Tracing your spiritual struggle through each of these nodes allows you to come to terms with the impact of divorce in each area. Ideally, reflection on and discussion about each area will move you toward greater health and a greater sense of control in your life. You also hope and believe that moving through each of these nodes allows you to process your divorce in all its complexity. There is no question that this process of spiritual discernment is difficult and sometimes treacherous. You struggle, resist, and run away. But ultimately, you grow. You find yourself renewed and strengthened. This does not happen all at once and may take years. As Mallory remarked to me, "You can't heal from everything all at once!" The point here is that if you remain conscious and reflective during these struggles, you will grow and flourish.

Coping with Trauma through Spirituality

Current research on spirituality and psychology shows that spirituality can help in coping with trauma if your spiritual outlook has a number of key qualities. According to Pargament, these include being *flexible, benevolent, integrated,* and *differentiated.* These characteristics speak to a complex, mature, and reflective spiritual outlook and we will examine each one. The stronger your spiritual life, the more you will gain from this journey. Also, while a strong spirituality can help you manage the struggles of divorce, those struggles, in turn, can strengthen your spirituality. This is a dynamic, mutually reinforcing process. Each of the chapters in this book has, I hope, coaxed you toward this type of spiritual outlook: a flexible system that is strong and resilient, without rigid or narrow beliefs that can leave you adrift and ill-equipped for the journey.

Flexibility

The narratives and life experiences you have read about in these pages show that growth in your spiritual life in the four areas mentioned above is quite common. You have seen several examples of increased *flexibility* in spiritual life, even when the stretching and shifting was challenging or painful. Flexibility means that your spiritual system is open to a variety of views about God and the divinely inspired life. It means that you are open to new perspectives and you are comfortable with change, when change is necessary. This is a position of epistemological humility, which means that you accept that your knowledge is limited or piecemeal when it comes to details about the realm of the Holy. Robin's perspective reflects this type of flexibility:

> I was born, raised, and confirmed into the Roman Catholic faith, and that is where I still attend mass most of the time. But I do not believe that access to God is the prerogative of any one institutional group, not Christian, Muslim, Jew, Hindu, Ba'hai, or worship of "the goddess." God cannot be owned or possessed or controlled … that is humans' domain—trying to "manage" God. Not possible … God does as God pleases.

Benevolence

Becoming more flexible in your spiritual views is a mark of maturity and positive development. During and after the divorce process, you may also come to a place of greater *benevolence* when thinking about God or the spiritual realm. Sometimes you open your heart to a wider and more loving understanding of the Divine. This happens as you come to experience grace and forgiveness in response to the ways you have fallen short of divine and personal expectations. Jolynn writes,

> I am gradually more open to the possibility that God is indeed my Beloved, and that no human being can love me in the unconditional way that God can. I have also come to realize that God is just as concerned about, or willing to be part of, the details and inconsequential aspects of my daily life as [God] is of the bigger life matters.

This open, loving view is the result of a long journey—a journey that Jolynn made through an unfamiliar landscape with pain as a companion. But she also had hope, which enabled her to keep moving forward toward a new horizon. Jessica's view of God also expanded as she made her way through divorce and reflects a spiritual life that has been renewed and reignited:

> I believe that God is aware of me, delights in me, tolerates, forgives, encourages, and loves me. That God's mercy and forgiveness is new every day. That God's love is endless and eternal and unconditional. I believe God understands humanity and its frailty. I believe that when I engage, God listens. I am aware of God's Holy Presence in my very being.

The move toward a more benevolent view of the Holy comes through sustained experiences of acceptance and grace. Words and experiences of grace come from a variety of sources—faithful partners on the journey, support groups, faith communities, and in your private times of contemplation and prayer. These experiences of grace go a long way toward bringing healing in ways that formal religious organizations have not always provided. If you have come to this more benevolent view of the Holy now, you can, in turn, act as a voice of grace for others.

Integration

We have seen throughout this book that divorce is a stripping-down process. You are in a new and frightening landscape, often very much against your will. But this stripping down also provides a unique opportunity—to investigate your life up to this point and to seek greater *integration*. This means making your life congruent so that your spiritual values and practices are threaded throughout all parts of your life. Your commitment to compassion should hold whether you speak to a friend or a stranger. Your embrace of transparency and honesty in your personal life should inform your professional life as well. As you move through this landscape, listening to your experience, you can decide what should stay as part of your life, and what should go. What brings you health and what brings you further suffering. What ignites your spiritual fire and what snuffs it out. You can take the healthy threads of your life and reweave them into a new pattern that exemplifies a life of love-in-action. If you are intentional and reflective and careful with your own heart, you can end up in a far healthier place, with an integrated spiritual life in which all aspects of yourself are in line and the life of the Holy breathes through all of it. Frances shows us what this looks like:

> I do feel I am living the life God called me to live, and it feels more a part of a whole rather than "my spiritual life," separate from the rest of my life. That doesn't mean I've "arrived" at some place and have no more to do. I think the difference now is the sense of contentment I feel about who I am and what I'm doing. To me, that's my spiritual life. It's not about certain spiritual practices— although they are important. It's more the coming together of all those things, and how all I've been and done informs the now, and how the now is more a deep-

ening of all that is and has been. I trust that what I have learned from my past is worth knowing, and that God trusts me to use what I have learned. I express my spiritual life in all I do ... or don't do. And I realize I still have plenty of growing and becoming in the years ahead. But at this point, there is a certain joy about that. Sort of like—what's next?

Part of a healthy sense of integration is recognizing how difficult it can be to remain conscious of your spiritual life when so many other things vie for your attention. When your life is truly integrated, you are aware of the spiritual reality of all life, and yet you also know that you must continue to work at listening to the voice of the Spirit within you. Karin puts it well by noting wryly about her relationship with God, "It's a struggle, kind of like dancing with a good lead when you have two left feet. It requires constant practice and intentionality, which come and go in spurts."

Differentiation

Not only may the aftermath of divorce lead to greater integration of your life, it may also lead to *differentiation* in your spiritual views. Differentiation refers to your ability to tolerate complexity (even paradox) and avoid the temptation of oversimplification. It also refers to how well you can accept new or challenging information. If your spirituality is well-differentiated, the dangers of the cul-de-sacs diminish and you grow in your ability to devise appropriate, creative, and healthy solutions to life's problems. Greater tolerance of complexity, ambiguity, and multiple approaches to God usually develop alongside a greater sense of mystery about the Divine. A greater embrace of mystery allows you to be genuinely humble, neither too big (arrogance) nor too small (self-denigration). It allows and encourages you to be more accepting of who you really are—both the good and the not-so-good. You become more open to the variety of ways God may work in your life, and you become more open to and accepting of your occasionally bumbling ways of responding to God. When asked how he saw his current relationship with God, Dan expressed both humility and hope:

> Honestly, I don't understand it. The story of the Nativity and the story of the Crucifixion are extremely powerful and resonate very strongly with me. Much of Jesus's ministry perplexes me. I am always full of thanks and wonder at the beauty of the earth and the astounding variety of Creation. I try to live by the golden rule and the teachings, and I am prepared to stand for judgment on the merits of my life. But on any given day I am petty and selfish and arrogant. Then, if I wake up the next day breathing, I've been given another chance.

Each of these aspects of your spiritual outlook—flexibility, benevolence, integration, differentiation—is important for maintaining a mature and growing spiritual life. Ultimately, the key to making it through this new landscape is openness—allowing your spirit to ask questions and ponder answers, to seek insights and reflect on suffering, to share your pain and listen to the voices of others on the same path. Janet showed me what this can look like:

> Searching for relief from emotional pain, I became a spiritual person. This took many years of personal study (books, classes, groups, trips, and research). This study often came from outside the Sunday visits and other required dates of the Catholic Church. Still, I often wrestle with what spirituality means. When I sit still long enough to really sink deep into the question, for me it means loving as Jesus did, respecting others without

judgment, forgiving even without being asked, and loving all the gifts we are given regardless of whether those gifts are tangible or intangible (such as "life lessons"). Not liking to ponder the painful lessons of my past, I'm not always grateful for them, but when I do revisit them I have lots to say and reflect upon. My heart yearns to feel unconditional love … and I wonder why I am not hearing a calling as others do; however, I do recognize that I have grown in [God's] spirit and for now that is enough.

Janet's openness of spirit allows her to continue moving forward, seeking God and the spiritual life. This ability to be open is based on a sense of hope and trust. When hope and trust reside in your heart, the Spirit can be reignited in your life. Jon's words resound with that same hope: "For me, my sense of relationship with God is based a lot on my understanding of who God is. I trust that whether or not I feel a personal closeness with God, God is up to something loving in the world and in my life."

Coming through the process of divorce should not be the culmination of your spiritual life, but only the beginning steps. Think how much you learn by walking on your own through this strange and unfamiliar landscape; by crafting a map and revising it as you go; by doing the reflection and self-assessment needed to avoid the cul-de-sacs and keep yourself moving in the right direction. Think of all the voices that have bolstered you, and all the voices that tried to hold you back. This is truly a remarkable thing! To see how far you have come and to see what you are actually capable of—this is a beginning, not an end. From this point on, you move forward with renewed inspiration. Because having made your way through, where you go next and what you do with all that "education of the heart" matters. Your task is not only to make it through the wilderness, but to help others find their way as well.

Questions for Reflection

1. How has your spiritual life shifted or changed while you were on this journey?

2. Can you detect greater integration, benevolence, differentiation, or flexibility in your spirituality? In what ways?

3. Have your views of God or the Holy changed? How?

4. What are three of the most important things you have learned while traversing this landscape?

5. How can you help others navigate through the landscape of divorce?

( )

A Prayer for Renewal

In this unfamiliar land, O God,
Grant me the courage to move forward, allowing hope to be my
companion.
Clear my vision and guide my steps along this new path.
When I am tempted to call myself a victim,
remind me that I am so much more,
and encourage me to embrace all of who I am.
When my heart claims that it is unlovable,
allow me to hear instead that I am imperfect
yet also made in your image, unique, and loved.
When I want to demonize others,
remind me of your regard for all people,
and cultivate respect in my heart.
When I swerve toward fearful isolation or hasty rebound,
lead me back to healthy community and grace-full solitude.
When I embrace judgmentalism,
pry my heart open and guide me toward forgiveness.
If I sink into bitterness,
let gratitude and your love buoy me to the surface.
Let your light shine in me, O God, as I walk this path.
May my hands, heart, and eyes be open,
and may I be a sign for others of love and of hope.
Amen.

CAROLYNE CALL

A Final Note

If You Are Considering Divorce

The decision to divorce is uniquely personal and the reasons behind it vary widely, based on each individual situation and circumstances. Sometimes there is very little you can do, as your spouse has already made the decision to leave and nothing you say or do makes a difference. Other times, you have made the decision to leave your spouse. While the ultimate decision must be made in response to your particular situation, there are a few things that can be said in general.

No one can make the final decision to divorce except you and your spouse. There are those who can help you in the process of discernment (a therapist or clergyperson, for example), but a decision of this magnitude must be made and owned by those who are living in the marriage. Only you know the deepest aspects of your marriage, including your history with your spouse. Only you know the nature and extent of any marital infractions, and only you can make an honest assessment of the potential for your future happiness.

A Last Resort

Having said that, divorce should be a last resort. Making a marriage succeed takes tremendous energy, self-reflection, communication, humility, and patience. Simply put, marriage is hard. A last resort means that every avenue for saving the marriage has been tried and has failed. This includes counseling, either individually, as a couple, or both. You come into marriage with expectations and goals, some of which are never verbalized. Counseling is one of the best ways to bring those expectations out into the open and to see if greater understanding can lead the marriage in a new, salvageable direction. Counseling can also help you, as individuals or as a couple, to understand yourself and to examine the issues or patterns you have brought to the marriage from your families of origin. Contrary to conventional wisdom, I believe that some people can change. Destructive or harmful patterns can be repaired and reconfigured, and you can transform your internal thoughts as well as your external behaviors and decisions. However, change only comes with hard work and commitment. It also only comes by personal choice. You cannot change anyone else—you can only change yourself.

If you are considering divorce, make sure you know exactly why you are considering it. This may seem obvious, but it is not as simple as it sounds. You may think you know the reasons, but you need to delve into the deeper reasons behind the reasons. So, for example, if you complain to your best friend that you want a divorce because you are unhappy, you need to know exactly what is causing your unhappiness. This is why counseling is critically important.

The decision to end a marriage (especially if there are children involved) should never be made lightly or without exploring what is happening under the surface. If you leave a marriage before understanding what has actually prompted the marital breakup, then you run the risk of repeating the same emotional mistakes in the future. You need to understand your role in the end of the marriage and take responsibility for that. This also means that you need to take time for this reflection and learning. If you are tempted to "bail out" and run, consider it a sign that something serious is happening that needs to be attended to and understood before you leave. You, your spouse, and your children (if any) will be the people living with the decision that you make. That means that you each must be willing to take responsibility for the decision you have made.

Finally, the decision to end a marriage should take some time. You stood before the judge or clergyperson and said your vows with the intention of keeping them. Your spouse did as well. For most of you, this was the most important promise you ever made to another person. If you have come to the point of questioning whether to remain married, you owe it to yourself as well as your spouse to take your time, exhaust all possibilities, and enter the process with as much care and consideration as possible.

( )

Appendix I

Group Formation and Discussion Guide

Setting Up a Spirituality of Divorce Reflection Group

Designing a Group

Leader(s) should do some advance planning for a group on spirituality and divorce. The following are suggested questions to consider when forming such a group. The more clearly you outline the group's goals and way of operating, the more effective the group will be.

What is the purpose of your group?

Reflect on all the possible goals and aspirations of the group you wish to create. Determining the group's goals will help to shape its structure and substance. Will it be purely for support purposes? Or do you want to add informational sessions? Do you want to create a group specifically for people currently going through the process of divorce? Or do you want to serve those who have already been through the process? Reflect carefully about what you hope to accomplish.

What will be the spiritual tone of the group?

In answering this question, you will shape the content and structure of the group. For example, is prayer a central practice or focus of the facilitator? If so, you might include prayer as an aspect of the meetings, or include exercises relating to prayer for the participants. What will be the spiritual orientation of the group? Are you hoping to attract people who are on the "margins" of your faith community or who may not consider themselves explicitly religious? If so, the type of religious language you use (or do not use) will be important.

What will be the structure of the group?

Here you're dealing with the nuts-and-bolts of the project. Consider carefully what the size of the group should be (limit it to twelve? ten?). Size affects group dynamics as well as trust and level of disclosure. Also think about who can join. Will this only be open to people within your own faith community or will you include those in the larger community as well? When will the group meet and for how long each time? Will this be an ongoing group or will it meet for a designated period (six weeks? six months?) Where will it meet?

What are the expectations for the group?

Two expectations should be clarified in advance so they can be communicated to the participants: confidentiality and attendance. Confidentiality is of crucial importance if the group is going to be designed for personal self-disclosure and support purposes. How you approach this depends on a variety of factors. For example, you may decide that confidentiality will be emphasized at the beginning and end of each session. Also consider how you will handle the situation if confidentiality is breached. In terms of attendance, you may wish to discuss with participants whether to establish an attendance policy. This may depend on the topics being covered or what the goal is for the group. Regular attendance takes on importance when the structure of a group involves personal self-disclosure and trust-building.

What support materials will the group use?

Facilitators can decide if they wish to use a book (like this one) as a means of guiding discussion in the group. You may also consider asking each participant to keep a journal. A journal is a useful way of integrating thoughts and reactions and may provide insights to the writer as well as to others when contents are (voluntarily) shared.

Once you have decided on how to structure the group you wish to host, you can move forward to implementation.

Setting Up the Group:

1. **Create a written description** of the group that can be handed out to prospective participants. This should include:

   - *The structure of the group.* This includes its size, how often it will meet, the time of day for the meetings, and where it will meet.
   - *The topics for the group.* Include what you will be discussing and whether you'll have outside speakers. Also mention if you'll be using a text.
   - *The requirements for the group.* Describe who can be a part of the group and what the expectations are for attendance.
   - *The role of confidentiality.*

2. **Recruit participants for the group.** Allow yourself at least four to six weeks to recruit interested participants. Spread the word through local channels, such as your faith community's newsletter, local newspapers, word of mouth, area counselors or retreat centers, and adult education programs.

3. *Prepare for your first meeting.* Be sure to pay attention to the setting of the room in which you will be meeting. This includes lighting, comfortable chairs, temperature, presence of food/drinks, background music, and other atmospheric conditions. (For example, can an office phone be heard in this room? Will it interrupt discussions?)

4. *Establish expectations.* While some ground rules should be established in advance (such as confidentiality), it is very helpful to ask the group as a whole to set their own ground rules for the sessions. For example, you can ask the group, "What should be the rule for cell phones while we're meeting?" or "Should there be restrictions on what kind of language we can use?"

5. *Conduct your meetings gracefully.* Keep in mind the key role of the facilitator—maintaining the flow of conversation, avoiding domination of the discussion by any one member, encouraging participation, recognizing important steps, and the like.

6. *Evaluation.* Prepare an evaluation, either in hard-copy form or online (through an outlet such as surveymonkey.com), and collect participant responses at the end of the program. This will enable you to improve your offerings in the future. You may also wish to conduct a verbal evaluation during one of the sessions halfway through the program.

Using This Book in a Group Setting

Here is a suggested outline for using this text for small group discussion over eight sessions. This procedure can be adjusted to fit your specific situation by adding more sessions or reducing the number by combining or skipping topics. Background is provided for the facilitators of the group and a list of suggested questions for discussion. Note also that participants can use the reflection questions at the close of each chapter for their own reflection or meditation as well. I encourage the use of a journal while participating in the group, since it allows for greater integration of the ideas and topics under discussion. Each session has explicit goals, exercises, and discussion topics. These can be modified to fit your group. At the end you will find a list of suggested rituals to use with your group.

Session 1: Humans as Spiritual Creatures

Reading Assignment: Introduction

Goal: Establish trust among members and reflect on where you have been.

Exercise: Create a spiritual timeline. Provide participants with sheets of paper, preferably at least 11" x 17". Ask participants to chart their spiritual lives from when they were children until now. This can be done with a linear type of graph, a spiral, a meandering pathway, or whatever seems most apt for their situation. Included in the spiritual timeline should be moments that stand out as times when their spiritual lives felt strong or cohesive, or when "things made sense" in a particular way. Also include the low points and times of confusion, faithlessness, or doubt.

Discussion Topics: What does your spiritual timeline tell you about your life up to this point? Do you see any patterns? Where does divorce fit? What are aspects of healthy spirituality? Who has served as a spiritual guide for you in the past?

Session 2: Divorce as a Spiritual Reality

Reading Assignment: Chapter 1

Goal: Make an explicit connection between the experience of divorce and your current spiritual life.

Exercise: Play word association exercises. The leader says specific words out loud and participants write down their immediate responses. The writing should be done in silence, without conversation among participants. Participants may also wish to sit in different parts of the room so their responses cannot be seen by others. The leader can reiterate the importance of writing down the first things that come to mind, even if they seem inappropriate or strange. Suggested words or phrases to use: wedding, diamond, my mother's view of marriage, vows, wife, husband, ceremony, sacred, society's view of marriage, mother-in-law, father-in-law, child, soul mate, wedding cake, marriage, divorce, faith, custody, broken, grief, etc. (The leader should add any others that he or she thinks would generate response for their particular group.)

Discussion Topics: What are your faith perspectives on divorce and what you have been taught? Were there any surprises in your word associations? What have you been taught about spirituality and marriage? How should we start thinking about spirituality and divorce? Explain the concept of a spiritual map.

Session 3: Spirituality and the Self

Reading Assignment: Chapters 2 and 3

Goal: Explore the effect of divorce on your self-esteem and identity.

Exercise: Initiate the finish-the-sentence exercise. Participants are provided with paper and pens. The leader instructs them to write out words to complete the sentences read out loud. Some suggested sentences (leader should include others):

> When I got married I was ...
> During our engagement I felt ...
> On my wedding day I ...
> My greatest accomplishment before I got married was ...
> When my spouse and I argued, I felt ...
> With my spouse's family I felt ...
> While I was married my friends ...
> During my marriage I loved doing ...
> While I was married I became very good at ...
> The time I felt the worst about myself was when ...
> I feel great when I ...
> In the last year I have learned to ...
> During my marriage my self-esteem ...

Discussion Topics: How has divorce changed your self-perception? What are the effects of divorce on your self-esteem? Are you a remaker or a regainer? What are new ways to build competence and self-value? What is your role in particular activities and relationships? The leader should show participants how to incorporate these insights into a spiritual map.

Session 4: Divorce and Relationships

Reading Assignment: Chapter 4; participants are asked to bring photographs of key people in their lives to the session.

Goal: Explore the effect of divorce on your personal relationships.

Exercise: Draw a relationship network before and after separation/divorce. Participants are provided with two large sheets of paper. On one sheet they draw a "web" illustrating their relationships while they were married. For example, in the center of the network would be the participant and his or her spouse, each in their own circle but enclosed within a larger circle. Draw lines out to other circles that would include family, friends, coworkers, and the like. For some relationships, the line would connect only one of the members of the marriage to another person (to a person's best friend, for example), while for others the lines would include both members of the marriage (to couples who are friends, or to family members). Draw a network on the second piece of paper representing the changed network following separation or divorce. Note where the major breaks have occurred, where new relationships have developed, and where changes in the intensity of relationships have occurred.

Discussion Topics: How have things changed in your relationships? What role roles do grief and loss play in this process? Which relationships might be saved and how?

Session 5: Spiritual Behaviors

Reading Assignment: Chapter 5

Goal: Honestly assess your own behavior during and after your divorce.

Exercise: Initiate honest self-appraisal. In this exercise participants are encouraged to reflect and write on their actions and choices during their marriage or at the end of their marriage. Each participant should have pen and paper. The leader will put the writing prompts on a piece of newsprint at the front of the room. Encourage everyone to find a comfortable place to write. You may wish to play meditative music in the background. Prompts should include:

> Every term I have used to describe my former spouse.
> One thing I did that was hurtful.
> A loving behavior I exhibited.
> One regret.
> One positive hope for my former spouse.

Discussion Topics: What are the behaviors of which you are most proud and most ashamed? How have you changed or modified your own behavior in different settings? How does spiritual life affect your behavior? What happens to you in the space between action and reaction? Revisit participants' spiritual maps.

Session 6: Divorce and Forgiveness

Reading Assignment: Chapter 6

Goal: Consider the role of self-forgiveness and other-forgiveness in your own situation.

Exercise: Write a third-person narrative of forgiveness. Each participant is provided with pen and paper. Ask each person to choose whether they will focus on self-forgiveness or forgiveness of another person. In the exercise the person writes out a narrative, from a third-person perspective, describing why the subject should be forgiven. For example, if I were focusing on self-forgiveness, I would write a narrative as if I were looking at myself from another person's perspective. That is, trying to be as objective about myself as possible. The narrative might run something like this: "I think Carolyne needs to be forgiven for her actions because when she was married she was somewhat immature and did not realize the impact her actions had ..." and so on. If I were to focus on my former spouse, I would write a narrative from the perspective of someone other than myself. That is, trying to see my spouse as an outsider would see him or her.

This is a very difficult exercise and participants may need some encouragement or suggestions. The goal is to step outside of ourselves in a very real way, and look at the situation and the people involved with a more objective eye. Some participants may find this impossible to do because of where they are on their personal journey with divorce. If this is the case, have them focus on writing out their responses to the questions, "What does forgiveness include?" and "When was a time I experienced forgiveness from another person?"

Discussion Topics: What is forgiveness? What is not forgiveness? Why is forgiveness so difficult (use case from text)? How might you approach this in your own life? What did you find when you tried to write out a narrative?

Session 7: God and Divorce

Reading Assignment: Chapter 7

Goal: Explore how divorce has changed or altered your perception of and relationship with God.

Exercise: God then and now. This exercise is similar to the finish-the-sentence exercise used previously, although participants should be encouraged to write more than one-word answers. Each participant should be provided with a pen and paper. Have everyone find a comfortable place to sit where they will feel comfortable writing responses. Write out the prompts on a piece of newsprint and display in the front of the room. Give participants enough time to write their answers in silence. Prompts could include some of the following:

> When I was a child I thought God was …
> When I was a child I thought God wanted me to …
> I learned about God from …
> My faith tradition saw marriage as …

During my marriage I believed …
My marriage and my spiritual life were …
During my marriage God was …
During my divorce God is/was …
When I found out I was getting divorced I thought God …
My faith right now is …
As an adult, I think God wants me to …
I no longer believe …

Discussion Topics: How has your relationship to God changed? What has had the greatest influence on the relationship? How is God calling you to live now?

Session 8: The Spiritually Healthy Divorce

Reading Assignment: Chapter 8

Goal: Reflect on the process of the class and how it has affected your understanding of your own divorce and spirituality.

Exercise: Share your spiritual map. Participants should have large pieces of paper and ample time to work undisturbed on their maps. Encourage them to draw the map in any style they choose. The map should include the following "features":

- What the horizon looks like
- Where the major obstacles are or have been (and names)
- Places we want to avoid
- Places where we can rest or regroup
- Signposts along the way
- Unexpected discoveries

Discussion Topics: What are the prominent features of your map? How have you made your way in the landscape? How has the journey changed your thinking and feeling? Where do you want to go from here?

Suggested Rituals
to Incorporate into
Group Sessions

Candle lighting: Using candles is an easy way to bring a sense of peace and sacredness to your time together with your participants. You may wish to have a single large candle that is lit at the beginning of each session and extinguished when the session ends. Or you may wish to have each participant hold a candle at the end of the session, and as the light is passed from one person to the next each speaks aloud a prayer request, a thought, or note of gratitude. There are endless possibilities for using candles in this type of setting.

Unison prayer: You may wish to open and/or close each session with a unison prayer from within your own faith tradition, or one you have written yourself. A unison prayer is an excellent opening and closing ritual because it reinforces a sense of unity within the group.

Circle prayer: This is a good ritual to use once the group has built some cohesion and connections. The leader (or a volunteer) initiates with a prayer and the prayer travels in a circle around the group. Participants speak aloud a prayer or wish for the person next to them. The leader closes with a brief prayer.

Forgiveness circle prayer: Everyone receives a slip of paper with "I pray/wish for forgiveness for …" and fills it in. The slips of paper are passed to the leader, who shuffles them then redistributes the slips of paper to the group. Participants read aloud what is on the paper they were given when the prayer circle begins. The leader closes with a brief prayer or leads a unison prayer.

Blessing of the journals: If the leader provides journals for use during the sessions, the leader can incorporate a blessing of the journals into the first session (usually at the close). This is simply a prayer said over the journals before they are distributed to participants. The leaders can compose a prayer, or use one like the following:

Gracious God, we ask for your blessing on these journals. May they be a place for healing, for insight, and for building courage. In our writing, let us see ourselves as you see us—with grace and with love. Amen.

Meditative music: Music can be used in a number of ways with a group. Music can be played while people arrive, helping to set an atmosphere. It can also be played while people are engaged in writing exercises. It may also be used for a time of meditation or prayer.

Silent prayer: Silent prayer allows participants the opportunity to name their own needs within their own minds and hearts. A candle can be used as a focusing device. The leader will need to close the time of prayer.

Narrative poetry exercise: This is an intensive and creative ritual that can have powerful results. Have the participants spend about ten minutes writing on a topic related to the discussion for that day. For example, at the second session you could ask them to write about "Times I felt the best about myself during my marriage." At the end of the allotted ten minutes, ask them to read back through what they have written and circle words or phrases that really stand out to them or that feel significant. Provide each participant with a small stack of paper scraps (varying in size from 1" x 1" to 1" x 3"). Have participants write out the circled words or phrases from the writing sample onto the scraps of paper (one word or phrase per scrap). Give each participant a 12" x 12" piece of scrapbook paper. On the scrapbook paper, encourage the participants to arrange and rearrange the scraps into a poem and then glue or tape the scraps in place. This exercise is intentionally abstract—the poem may not have a traditional format or phrasing, but will have personal meaning to the person who makes it. Remind them that there is no *right way* to complete this exercise. It is intended to help us think and reflect in different ways and to offer a new perspective on the topic under discussion. The poems may be shared during a closing time of prayer/reflection if participants wish to.

Letters to self: An excellent ritual for closing a discussion group is to give participants about ten minutes to write themselves a letter. This letter will be put into a sealed envelope, addressed, and mailed to the participant either six months or a year from the last session. (The leaders decides on the time interval.) The letter should speak to what the person has come to learn during the sessions, what they wish for themselves for the future, and what they are committing to working on for the next six months (or year). After the letters are written they can be placed on a table in the center of the closing circle of prayer.

Suggestions for Further Reading

If you are facing divorce, there are, of course, myriad books available that address a wide range of topics such as the current research on the effects of divorce on children, legal issues, and financial concerns. There are also many resources for personal growth that you may find helpful during this challenging time. While the following list is in no way comprehensive, you may find these resources helpful, informative and, in many cases, comforting.

Divorce or Dealing with Life after Divorce

Instone-Brewer, David. *Divorce and Remarriage in the Church: Biblical Solutions for Pastoral Realities* Nottingham, UK: Inter-Varsity Press, 2006.

Netter, Perry. *Divorce Is a Mitzvah: A Practical Guide to Finding Wholeness and Holiness When Your Marriage Dies*. Woodstock, VT: Jewish Lights Publishing, 2002.

Root, Andrew. *Children of Divorce: The Loss of Family as the Loss of Being*. Grand Rapids, MI: Baker Academic, 2010.

Forgiveness

Enright, Robert D. *Forgiveness Is a Choice: A Step-by-Step Process for Resolving Anger and Restoring Hope*. Washington, DC: American Psychological Association, 2001.

Ford, Marcia. *The Sacred Art of Forgiveness: Finding Ourselves and Others through God's Grace*. Woodstock, VT: SkyLight Paths Publishing, 2006.

Kedar, Karyn D. *A Bridge to Forgiveness: Stories and Prayers for Finding God and Restoring Wholeness*. Woodstock, VT: Jewish Lights Publishing, 2010.

Spiritual Living and Personal Growth

Bieber, Nancy. *Decision Making and Spiritual Discernment: The Sacred Art of Finding Your Way*. Woodstock, VT: SkyLight Paths Publishing, 2010.

Copeland-Payton, Nancy. *The Losses of Our Lives: The Sacred Gifts of Renewal in Everyday Loss*. Woodstock, VT: SkyLight Paths Publishing, 2011.

Dalai Lama. *The Good Heart: A Buddhist Perspective on the Teachings of Jesus*. Somerville, MA: Wisdom Publications, 1998.

———. *How to See Yourself as You Really Are*. New York: Atria, 2007.

DeMello, Anthony. *Awareness: The Perils and Opportunities of Reality*. Garden City, NY: Image, 1990.

Frankl, Viktor. *Man's Search for Meaning*. Boston: Beacon Press, 2006.

Goldstein, Niles Elliot. *The Challenge of the Soul: A Guide for the Spiritual Warrior*. Boston: Trumpeter, 2009.

Homan, Daniel, and Lonni Collins Pratt. *Radical Hospitality: Benedict's Way of Love*. Orleans, MA: Paraclete Press, 2002.

Lerner, Harriet. *The Dance of Anger: A Woman's Guide to Changing the Patterns of Intimate Relationships*. New York, Harper Paperbacks, 2005.

———. *The Dance of Connections: How to Talk to Someone When You're Mad, Hurt, Scared, Frustrated, Insulted, Betrayed, or Desperate*. New York: Harper Paperbacks, 2002.

———. *The Dance of Intimacy*. New York: Harper Paperback, 1990.

Lamott, Anne. *Traveling Mercies: Some Thoughts on Faith*. New York: Anchor, 2000.

McCullough, Michael E., Kenneth I. Pargament, and Carl E. Thoresen, eds. *Forgiveness: Theory, Research, and Practice*. New York: Guilford Press, 2001.

Miles, Sara. *Take This Bread: A Radical Conversion*. New York: Ballantine Books, 2008.

Mosteller, Sue. *Light through the Crack: Life after Loss*. New York: Doubleday, 2006.

Palmer, Parker. *A Hidden Wholeness: The Journey Toward an Undivided Life*. San Francisco: Jossey-Bass, 2009.

———. *Let Your Life Speak: Listening for the Voice of Vocation*. San Francisco: Jossey-Bass, 1999.

Pargament, Kenneth. *The Psychology of Religion and Coping*. New York: Guilford Press, 2001.

Taylor, Barbara Brown. *An Altar in the World: A Geography of Faith*. New York: HarperOne, 2010.

Peerman, Gordon. *Blessed Relief: What Christians Can Learn from Buddhists about Suffering*. Woodstock, VT: SkyLight Paths Publishing, 2009.

Rinpoche, Yongey Mingyur, and Eric Swanson. *Joyful Wisdom: Embracing Change and Finding Freedom* (Three Rivers Press, 2010)

Sparks, Susan. *Laugh Your Way to Grace: Reclaiming the Spiritual Power of Humor*. Woodstock, VT. SkyLight Paths Publishing, 2010.

Taylor, Terry. *A Spirituality for Brokenness: Discovering Your Deepest Self in Difficult Times*. Woodstock, VT: SkyLight Paths Publishing, 2009.

Children's Spirituality—Board Books

Adam & Eve's New Day
by Sandy Eisenberg Sasso; Full-color illus. by Joani Keller Rothenberg
A lesson in hope for every child who has worried about what comes next. Abridged from *Adam & Eve's First Sunset*.
5 x 5, 24 pp, Full-color illus., Board Book, 978-1-59473-205-8 **$7.99** *For ages 0–4*

How Did the Animals Help God?
by Nancy Sohn Swartz; Full-color illus. by Melanie Hall
God asks all of nature to offer gifts to humankind—with a promise that they will care for creation in return. Abridged from *In Our Image*.
5 x 5, 24 pp, Full-color illus., Board Book, 978-1-59473-044-3 **$7.99** *For ages 0–4*

How Does God Make Things Happen?
by Lawrence and Karen Kushner; Full-color illus. by Dawn W. Majewski
A charming invitation for young children to explore how God makes things happen in our world. Abridged from *Because Nothing Looks Like God*.
5 x 5, 24 pp, Full-color illus., Board Book, 978-1-893361-24-9 **$7.95** *For ages 0–4*

What Does God Look Like?
by Lawrence and Karen Kushner; Full-color illus. by Dawn W. Majewski
A simple way for young children to explore the ways that we "see" God. Abridged from *Because Nothing Looks Like God*.
5 x 5, 24 pp, Full-color illus., Board Book, 978-1-893361-23-2 **$7.99** *For ages 0–4*

What Is God's Name?
by Sandy Eisenberg Sasso; Full-color illus. by Phoebe Stone
Everyone and everything in the world has a name. What is God's name? Abridged from the award-winning *In God's Name*.
5 x 5, 24 pp, Full-color illus., Board Book, 978-1-893361-10-2 **$7.99** *For ages 0–4*

Where Is God?
by Lawrence and Karen Kushner; Full-color illus. by Dawn W. Majewski
A gentle way for young children to explore how God is with us every day, in every way. Abridged from *Because Nothing Looks Like God*.
5 x 5, 24 pp, Full-color illus., Board Book, 978-1-893361-17-1 **$7.99** *For ages 0–4*

Or phone, fax, mail or e-mail to: SKYLIGHT PATHS Publishing
Sunset Farm Offices, Route 4 • P.O. Box 237 • Woodstock, Vermont 05091
Tel: (802) 457-4000 • Fax: (802) 457-4004 • www.skylightpaths.com
Credit card orders: (800) 962-4544 (8:30AM–5:30PM ET Monday–Friday)
Generous discounts on quantity orders. SATISFACTION GUARANTEED. Prices subject to change.

Children's Spirituality

Remembering My Grandparent: A Kid's Own Grief Workbook in the Christian Tradition *by Nechama Liss-Levinson, PhD, and Rev. Molly Phinney Baskette, MDiv* 8 x 10, 48 pp, 2-color text, HC, 978-1-59473-212-6 **$16.99** *For ages 7 & up*

Does God Ever Sleep? *by Joan Sauro, CSJ*
A charming nighttime reminder that God is always present in our lives.
10 x 8½, 32 pp, Full-color photos, Quality PB, 978-1-59473-110-5 **$8.99** *For ages 3–6*

Does God Forgive Me? *by August Gold; Full-color photos by Diane Hardy Waller*
Gently shows how God forgives all that we do if we are truly sorry.
10 x 8½, 32 pp, Full-color photos, Quality PB, 978-1-59473-142-6 **$8.99** *For ages 3–6*

God Said Amen *by Sandy Eisenberg Sasso; Full-color illus. by Avi Katz*
A warm and inspiring tale that shows us that we need only reach out to each other to find the answers to our prayers.
9 x 12, 32 pp. Full-color illus., HC, 978-1-58023-080-3 **$16.95*** *For ages 4 & up*

How Does God Listen? *by Kay Lindahl; Full-color photos by Cynthia Maloney*
How do we know when God is listening to us? Children will find the answers to these questions as they engage their senses while the story unfolds, learning how God listens in the wind, waves, clouds, hot chocolate, perfume, our tears and our laughter.
10 x 8½, 32 pp, Full-color photos, Quality PB, 978-1-59473-084-9 **$8.99** *For ages 3–6*

In God's Hands *by Lawrence Kushner and Gary Schmidt; Full-color illus. by Matthew J. Baek*
9 x 12, 32 pp, Full-color illus., HC, 978-1-58023-224-1 **$16.99*** *For ages 5 & up*

In God's Name *by Sandy Eisenberg Sasso; Full-color illus. by Phoebe Stone*
Like an ancient myth in its poetic text and vibrant illustrations, this award-winning modern fable about the search for God's name celebrates the diversity and, at the same time, the unity of all the people of the world.
9 x 12, 32 pp, Full-color illus., HC, 978-1-879045-26-2 **$16.99*** *For ages 4 & up*

Also available in Spanish: **El nombre de Dios**
9 x 12, 32 pp, Full-color illus., HC, 978-1-893361-63-8 **$16.95**

In Our Image: God's First Creatures
by Nancy Sohn Swartz; Full-color illus. by Melanie Hall
A playful new twist on the Genesis story—from the perspective of the animals. Celebrates the interconnectedness of nature and the harmony of all living things.
9 x 12, 32 pp, Full-color illus., HC, 978-1-879045-99-6 **$16.95*** *For ages 4 & up*

Noah's Wife: The Story of Naamah
by Sandy Eisenberg Sasso; Full-color illus. by Bethanne Andersen
Opens young readers' religious imaginations to new ideas about the well-known story of the Flood. When God tells Noah to bring the animals of the world onto the ark, God also calls on Naamah, Noah's wife, to save each plant on Earth.
9 x 12, 32 pp, Full-color illus., HC, 978-1-58023-134-3 **$16.95*** *For ages 4 & up*

Also available: **Naamah:** Noah's Wife (A Board Book)
by Sandy Eisenberg Sasso; Full-color illus. by Bethanne Andersen
5 x 5, 24 pp, Full-color illus., Board Book, 978-1-893361-56-0 **$7.95** *For ages 0–4*

Where Does God Live? *by August Gold and Matthew J. Perlman*
Helps children and their parents find God in the world around us with simple, practical examples children can relate to.
10 x 8½, 32 pp, Full-color photos, Quality PB, 978-1-893361-39-3 **$8.99** *For ages 3–6*

* A book from Jewish Lights, SkyLight Paths' sister imprint

Children's Spirituality

Adam & Eve's First Sunset: God's New Day
by Sandy Eisenberg Sasso; Full-color illus. by Joani Keller Rothenberg 9 x 12, 32 pp, Full-color illus., HC, 978-1-58023-177-0 **$17.95*** *For ages 4 & up*

Because Nothing Looks Like God
by Lawrence Kushner and Karen Kushner; Full-color illus. by Dawn W. Majewski
Invites parents and children to explore the questions we all have about God.
11 x 8½, 32 pp, Full-color illus., HC, 978-1-58023-092-6 **$17.99*** *For ages 4 & up*
Also available: **Teacher's Guide** 8½ x 11, 22 pp, PB, 978-1-58023-140-4 **$6.95** *For ages 5–8*

But God Remembered: Stories of Women from Creation to the Promised Land *by Sandy Eisenberg Sasso; Full-color illus. by Bethanne Andersen*
A fascinating collection of four different stories of women only briefly mentioned in biblical tradition and religious texts.
9 x 12, 32 pp, Full-color illus., Quality PB, 978-1-58023-372-9 **$8.99*** *For ages 8 & up*

Cain & Abel: Finding the Fruits of Peace
by Sandy Eisenberg Sasso; Full-color illus. by Joani Keller Rothenberg
A sensitive recasting of the ancient tale shows we have the power to deal with anger in positive ways. "Editor's Choice." —American Library Association's *Booklist*
9 x 12, 32 pp, Full-color illus., HC, 978-1-58023-123-7 **$16.95*** *For ages 5 & up*

Does God Hear My Prayer?
by August Gold; Full-color photos by Diane Hardy Waller
Introduces preschoolers and young readers to prayer and how it helps them express their own emotions.
10 x 8½, 32 pp, Full-color photo illus., Quality PB, 978-1-59473-102-0 **$8.99** *For ages 3–6*

The 11th Commandment: Wisdom from Our Children *by The Children of America*
"If there were an Eleventh Commandment, what would it be?" Children of many religious denominations across America answer this question—in their own drawings and words. "A rare book of spiritual celebration for all people, of all ages, for all time." —*Bookviews* 8 x 10, 48 pp, Full-color illus., HC, 978-1-879045-46-0 **$16.95*** *For all ages*

For Heaven's Sake *by Sandy Eisenberg Sasso; Full-color illus. by Kathryn Kunz Finney*
Heaven is often found where you least expect it.
9 x 12, 32 pp, Full-color illus., HC, 978-1-58023-054-4 **$16.95*** *For ages 4 & up*

God in Between *by Sandy Eisenberg Sasso; Full-color illus. by Sally Sweetland*
A magical, mythical tale that teaches that God can be found where we are.
9 x 12, 32 pp, Full-color illus., HC, 978-1-879045-86-6 **$16.95*** *For ages 4 & up*

God's Paintbrush: Special 10th Anniversary Edition
Invites children of all faiths and backgrounds to encounter God through moments in their own lives. 11 x 8½, 32 pp, Full-color illus., HC, 978-1-58023-195-4 **$17.95*** *For ages 4 & up*
Also available: **God's Paintbrush Teacher's Guide**
8½ x 11, 32 pp, PB, 978-1-879045-57-6 **$8.95**
God's Paintbrush Celebration Kit: A Spiritual Activity Kit for Teachers and Students of All Faiths, All Backgrounds 9½ x 12, 40 Full-color Activity Sheets & Teacher Folder w/ complete instructions, HC, 978-1-58023-050-6 **$21.95**
Additional activity sheets available:
8-Student Activity Sheet Pack (40 sheets/5 sessions), 978-1-58023-058-2 **$19.95**
Single-Student Activity Sheet Pack (5 sessions), 978-1-58023-059-9 **$3.95**

I Am God's Paintbrush (A Board Book)
by Sandy Eisenberg Sasso; Full-color illus. by Annette Compton
5 x 5, 24 pp, Full-color illus., Board Book, 978-1-59473-265-2 **$7.99** *For ages 0–4*

* A book from Jewish Lights, SkyLight Paths' sister imprint

Spiritual Poetry—The Mystic Poets

Experience these mystic poets as you never have before. Each beautiful, compact book includes a brief introduction to the poet's time and place, a summary of the major themes of the poet's mysticism and religious tradition, essential selections from the poet's most important works, and an appreciative preface by a contemporary spiritual writer.

Hafiz
The Mystic Poets
Translated and with Notes by Gertrude Bell
Preface by Ibrahim Gamard
Hafiz is known throughout the world as Persia's greatest poet, with sales of his poems in Iran today only surpassed by those of the Qur'an itself. His probing and joyful verse speaks to people from all backgrounds who long to taste and feel divine love and experience harmony with all living things.
5 x 7¼, 144 pp, HC, 978-1-59473-009-2 **$16.99**

Hopkins
The Mystic Poets
Preface by Rev. Thomas Ryan, CSP
Gerard Manley Hopkins, Christian mystical poet, is beloved for his use of fresh language and startling metaphors to describe the world around him. Although his verse is lovely, beneath the surface lies a searching soul, wrestling with and yearning for God.
5 x 7¼, 112 pp, HC, 978-1-59473-010-8 **$16.99**

Tagore
The Mystic Poets
Preface by Swami Adiswarananda
Rabindranath Tagore is often considered the Shakespeare of modern India. A great mystic, Tagore was the teacher of W. B. Yeats and Robert Frost, the close friend of Albert Einstein and Mahatma Gandhi, and the winner of the Nobel Prize for Literature. This beautiful sampling of Tagore's two most important works, *The Gardener* and *Gitanjali,* offers a glimpse into his spiritual vision that has inspired people around the world.
5 x 7¼, 144 pp, HC, 978-1-59473-008-5 **$16.99**

Whitman
The Mystic Poets
Preface by Gary David Comstock
Walt Whitman was the most innovative and influential poet of the nineteenth century. This beautiful sampling of Whitman's most important poetry from *Leaves of Grass,* and selections from his prose writings, offers a glimpse into the spiritual side of his most radical themes—love for country, love for others and love of self.
5 x 7¼, 192 pp, HC, 978-1-59473-041-2 **$16.99**

Journeys of Simplicity
Traveling Light with Thomas Merton, Bashō,
Edward Abbey, Annie Dillard & Others
by Philip Harnden
Invites you to consider a more graceful way of traveling through life.
PB includes journal pages to help you get started on
your own spiritual journey.
5 x 7¼, 144 pp, Quality PB, 978-1-59473-181-5 **$12.99**
5 x 7¼, 128 pp, HC, 978-1-893361-76-8 **$16.95**

Judaism / Christianity / Islam / Interfaith

Getting to the Heart of Interfaith

The Eye-Opening, Hope-Filled Friendship of a Pastor, a Rabbi and a Sheikh
by Pastor Don Mackenzie, Rabbi Ted Falcon and Sheikh Jamal Rahman
Offers many insights and encouragements for individuals and groups who want to tap into the promise of interfaith dialogue. 6 x 9, 192 pp, Quality PB, 978-1-59473-263-8 **$16.99**

Hearing the Call across Traditions: Readings on Faith and Service

Edited by Adam Davis; Foreword by Eboo Patel Explores the connections between faith, service and social justice through the prose, verse and sacred texts of the world's great faith traditions. 6 x 9, 352 pp, HC, 978-1-59473-264-5 **$29.99**

How to Do Good & Avoid Evil: A Global Ethic from the Sources of

Judaism *by Hans Küng and Rabbi Walter Homolka; Translated by Rev. Dr. John Bowden*
Explores how Judaism's ethical principles can help all religions work together toward a more peaceful humankind. 6 x 9, 224 pp, HC, 978-1-59473-255-3 **$19.99**

Blessed Relief: What Christians Can Learn from Buddhists about Suffering
by Gordon Peerman 6 x 9, 208 pp, Quality PB, 978-1-59473-252-2 **$16.99**

The Changing Christian World: A Brief Introduction for Jews
by Rabbi Leonard A. Schoolman 5½ x 8½, 176 pp, Quality PB, 978-1-58023-344-6 **$16.99***

Christians & Jews in Dialogue: Learning in the Presence of the Other *by Mary C. Boys and Sara S. Lee; Foreword by Dorothy C. Bass* 6 x 9, 240 pp, Quality PB, 978-1-59473-254-6 **$18.99**; HC, 978-1-59473-144-0 **$21.99**

Disaster Spiritual Care: Practical Clergy Responses to Community, Regional and National Tragedy *Edited by Rabbi Stephen B. Roberts, BCJC, and Rev. Willard W.C. Ashley, Sr., DMin, DH* 6 x 9, 384 pp, HC, 978-1-59473-240-9 **$40.00**

InterActive Faith: The Essential Interreligious Community-Building Handbook
Edited by Rev. Bud Heckman with Rori Picker Neiss; Foreword by Rev. Dirk Ficca
6 x 9, 304 pp, HC, 978-1-59473-237-9 **$29.99**

The Jewish Approach to God: A Brief Introduction for Christians
by Rabbi Neil Gillman, PhD 5½ x 8½, 192 pp, Quality PB, 978-1-58023-190-9 **$16.95***

The Jewish Approach to Repairing the World (*Tikkun Olam*): A Brief Introduction for Christians *by Rabbi Elliot N. Dorff, PhD, with Rev. Cory Willson*
5½ x 8½, 256 pp, Quality PB, 978-1-58023-349-1 **$16.99***

The Jewish Connection to Israel, the Promised Land: A Brief Introduction for Christians *by Rabbi Eugene Korn, PhD* 5½ x 8½, 192 pp, Quality PB, 978-1-58023-318-7 **$14.99***

Jewish Holidays: A Brief Introduction for Christians *by Rabbi Kerry M. Olitzky and Rabbi Daniel Judson* 5½ x 8½, 176 pp, Quality PB, 978-1-58023-302-6 **$16.99***

Jewish Ritual: A Brief Introduction for Christians
by Rabbi Kerry M. Olitzky and Rabbi Daniel Judson 5½ x 8½, 144 pp, Quality PB, 978-1-58023-210-4 **$14.99***

Jewish Spirituality: A Brief Introduction for Christians *by Rabbi Lawrence Kushner*
5½ x 8½, 112 pp, Quality PB, 978-1-58023-150-3 **$12.95***

A Jewish Understanding of the New Testament *by Rabbi Samuel Sandmel;*
New preface by Rabbi David Sandmel 5½ x 8½, 368 pp, Quality PB, 978-1-59473-048-1 **$19.99***

Modern Jews Engage the New Testament: Enhancing Jewish Well-Being in a Christian Environment *by Rabbi Michael J. Cook, PhD* 6 x 9, 416 pp, HC 978-1-58023-313-2 **$29.99***

Talking about God: Exploring the Meaning of Religious Life with Kierkegaard, Buber, Tillich and Heschel *by Daniel F. Polish, PhD* 6 x 9, 160 pp, Quality PB, 978-1-59473-272-0 **$16.99**

We Jews and Jesus: Exploring Theological Differences for Mutual Understanding
by Rabbi Samuel Sandmel; New preface by Rabbi David Sandmel
6 x 9, 192 pp, Quality PB, 978-1-59473-208-9 **$16.99**

Who Are the *Real* Chosen People? The Meaning of Chosenness in Judaism, Christianity and Islam *by Reuven Firestone, PhD*
6 x 9, 176 pp, Quality PB, 978-1-59473-290-4 **$16.99**

* A book from Jewish Lights, SkyLight Paths' sister imprint

Bible Stories / Folktales

Abraham's Bind & Other Bible Tales of Trickery, Folly, Mercy and Love *by Michael J. Caduto*
New retellings of episodes in the lives of familiar biblical characters explore relevant life lessons.   6 x 9, 224 pp, HC, 978-1-59473-186-0 **$19.99**

Daughters of the Desert: Stories of Remarkable Women from Christian, Jewish and Muslim Traditions *by Claire Rudolf Murphy, Meghan Nuttall Sayres, Mary Cronk Farrell, Sarah Conover and Betsy Wharton*
Breathes new life into the old tales of our female ancestors in faith. Uses traditional scriptural passages as starting points, then with vivid detail fills in historical context and place. Chapters reveal the voices of Sarah, Hagar, Huldah, Esther, Salome, Mary Magdalene, Lydia, Khadija, Fatima and many more. Historical fiction ideal for readers of all ages.
5½ x 8½, 192 pp, Quality PB, 978-1-59473-106-8 **$14.99**   Inc. reader's discussion guide
HC, 978-1-893361-72-0 **$19.95**

The Triumph of Eve & Other Subversive Bible Tales
by Matt Biers-Ariel
These engaging retellings of familiar Bible stories are witty, often hilarious and always profound. They invite you to grapple with questions and issues that are often hidden in the original texts.
5½ x 8½, 192 pp, Quality PB, 978-1-59473-176-1 **$14.99**
Also available: **The Triumph of Eve Teacher's Guide**
8½ x 11, 44 pp, PB, 978-1-59473-152-5 **$8.99**

Wisdom in the Telling
Finding Inspiration and Grace in Traditional Folktales and Myths Retold
by Lorraine Hartin-Gelardi
6 x 9, 192 pp, HC, 978-1-59473-185-3 **$19.99**

Religious Etiquette / Reference

How to Be a Perfect Stranger, 4th Edition: The Essential Religious Etiquette Handbook *Edited by Stuart M. Matlins and Arthur J. Magida*
The indispensable guidebook to help the well-meaning guest when visiting other people's religious ceremonies. A straightforward guide to the rituals and celebrations of the major religions and denominations in the United States and Canada from the perspective of an interested guest of any other faith, based on information obtained from authorities of each religion. Belongs in every living room, library and office. Covers:
African American Methodist Churches • Assemblies of God • Bahá'í • Baptist • Buddhist • Christian Church (Disciples of Christ) • Christian Science (Church of Christ, Scientist) • Churches of Christ • Episcopalian and Anglican • Hindu • Islam • Jehovah's Witnesses • Jewish • Lutheran • Mennonite/Amish • Methodist • Mormon (Church of Jesus Christ of Latter-day Saints) • Native American/First Nations • Orthodox Churches • Pentecostal Church of God • Presbyterian • Quaker (Religious Society of Friends) • Reformed Church in America/Canada • Roman Catholic • Seventh-day Adventist • Sikh • Unitarian Universalist • United Church of Canada • United Church of Christ

"The things Miss Manners forgot to tell us about religion."
—*Los Angeles Times*

"Finally, for those inclined to undertake their own spiritual journeys ... tells visitors what to expect." —*New York Times*
6 x 9, 432 pp, Quality PB, 978-1-59473-140-2 **$19.99**

The Perfect Stranger's Guide to Funerals and Grieving Practices: A Guide to Etiquette in Other People's Religious Ceremonies *Edited by Stuart M. Matlins*
6 x 9, 240 pp, Quality PB, 978-1-893361-20-1 **$16.95**

The Perfect Stranger's Guide to Wedding Ceremonies: A Guide to Etiquette in Other People's Religious Ceremonies *Edited by Stuart M. Matlins*
6 x 9, 208 pp, Quality PB, 978-1-893361-19-5 **$16.95**

Spirituality of the Seasons

Autumn: A Spiritual Biography of the Season
Edited by Gary Schmidt and Susan M. Felch; Illus. by Mary Azarian
Rejoice in autumn as a time of preparation and reflection. Includes Wendell Berry, David James Duncan, Robert Frost, A. Bartlett Giamatti, E. B. White, P. D. James, Julian of Norwich, Garret Keizer, Tracy Kidder, Anne Lamott, May Sarton.
6 x 9, 320 pp, b/w illus., Quality PB, 978-1-59473-118-1 **$18.99**

Spring: A Spiritual Biography of the Season
Edited by Gary Schmidt and Susan M. Felch; Illus. by Mary Azarian
Explore the gentle unfurling of spring and reflect on how nature celebrates rebirth and renewal. Includes Jane Kenyon, Lucy Larcom, Harry Thurston, Nathaniel Hawthorne, Noel Perrin, Annie Dillard, Martha Ballard, Barbara Kingsolver, Dorothy Wordsworth, Donald Hall, David Brill, Lionel Basney, Isak Dinesen, Paul Laurence Dunbar. 6 x 9, 352 pp, b/w illus., Quality PB, 978-1-59473-246-1 **$18.99**

Summer: A Spiritual Biography of the Season
Edited by Gary Schmidt and Susan M. Felch; Illus. by Barry Moser
"A sumptuous banquet…. These selections lift up an exquisite wholeness found within an everyday sophistication." — ★ *Publishers Weekly* starred review
Includes Anne Lamott, Luci Shaw, Ray Bradbury, Richard Selzer, Thomas Lynch, Walt Whitman, Carl Sandburg, Sherman Alexie, Madeleine L'Engle, Jamaica Kincaid.
6 x 9, 304 pp, b/w illus., Quality PB, 978-1-59473-183-9 **$18.99**
HC, 978-1-59473-083-2 **$21.99**

Winter: A Spiritual Biography of the Season
Edited by Gary Schmidt and Susan M. Felch; Illus. by Barry Moser
"This outstanding anthology features top-flight nature and spirituality writers on the fierce, inexorable season of winter…. Remarkably lively and warm, despite the icy subject." — ★ *Publishers Weekly* starred review
Includes Will Campbell, Rachel Carson, Annie Dillard, Donald Hall, Ron Hansen, Jane Kenyon, Jamaica Kincaid, Barry Lopez, Kathleen Norris, John Updike, E. B. White.
6 x 9, 288 pp, b/w illus., Deluxe PB w/ flaps, 978-1-893361-92-8 **$18.95**;
HC, 978-1-893361-53-9 **$21.95**

Spirituality / Animal Companions

Blessing the Animals: Prayers and Ceremonies to Celebrate God's Creatures, Wild and Tame *Edited and with Introductions by Lynn L. Caruso*
5¼ x 7¼, 256 pp, Quality PB, 978-1-59473-253-9 **$15.99**; HC, 978-1-59473-145-7 **$19.99**

Remembering My Pet: A Kid's Own Spiritual Workbook for When a Pet Dies
by Nechama Liss-Levinson, PhD, and Rev. Molly Phinney Baskette, MDiv; Foreword by Lynn L. Caruso
8 x 10, 48 pp, 2-color text, HC, 978-1-59473-221-8 **$16.99**

What Animals Can Teach Us about Spirituality: Inspiring Lessons from Wild and Tame Creatures *by Diana L. Guerrero* 6 x 9, 176 pp, Quality PB, 978-1-893361-84-3 **$16.95**

Spirituality—A Week Inside

Lighting the Lamp of Wisdom: A Week Inside a Yoga Ashram
by John Ittner; Foreword by Dr. David Frawley
6 x 9, 192 pp, b/w photos, Quality PB, 978-1-893361-52-2 **$15.95**

Making a Heart for God: A Week Inside a Catholic Monastery
by Dianne Aprile; Foreword by Brother Patrick Hart, OCSO
6 x 9, 224 pp, b/w photos, Quality PB, 978-1-893361-49-2 **$16.95**

Waking Up: A Week Inside a Zen Monastery
by Jack Maguire; Foreword by John Daido Loori, Roshi
6 x 9, 224 pp, b/w photos, Quality PB, 978-1-893361-55-3 **$16.95**; HC, 978-1-893361-13-3 **$21.95**

Spirituality

Creative Aging: Rethinking Retirement and Non-Retirement in a Changing World   *by Marjory Zoet Bankson*
Offers creative ways to nourish our calling and discover meaning and purpose in our older years.   6 x 9, 160 pp, Quality PB, 978-1-59473-281-2 **$16.99**

Laugh Your Way to Grace: Reclaiming the Spiritual Power of Humor
by Rev. Susan Sparks   A powerful, humorous case for laughter as a spiritual, healing path.   6 x 9, 176 pp, Quality PB, 978-1-59473-280-5 **$16.99**

Living into Hope: A Call to Spiritual Action for Such a Time as This
by Rev. Dr. Joan Brown Campbell; Foreword by Karen Armstrong
A visionary minister speaks out on the pressing issues that face us today, offering inspiration and challenge.   6 x 9, 144 pp (est), HC, 978-1-59473-283-6 **$21.99**

Claiming Earth as Common Ground: The Ecological Crisis through the Lens of Faith   *by Andrea Cohen-Kiener; Foreword by Rev. Sally Bingham*
Inspires us to work across denominational lines in order to fulfill our sacred imperative to care for God's creation.   6 x 9, 192 pp, Quality PB, 978-1-59473-261-4 **$16.99**

Bread, Body, Spirit: Finding the Sacred in Food
Edited and with Introductions by Alice Peck   6 x 9, 224 pp, Quality PB, 978-1-59473-242-3 **$19.99**

Creating a Spiritual Retirement: A Guide to the Unseen Possibilities in Our Lives
by Molly Srode   6 x 9, 208 pp, b/w photos, Quality PB, 978-1-59473-050-4 **$14.99**

Finding Hope: Cultivating God's Gift of a Hopeful Spirit
by Marcia Ford; Foreword by Andrea Jaeger   8 x 8, 176 pp, Quality PB, 978-1-59473-211-9 **$16.99**

Hearing the Call across Traditions: Readings on Faith and Service
Edited by Adam Davis; Foreword by Eboo Patel   6 x 9, 352 pp, HC, 978-1-59473-264-5 **$29.99**

Honoring Motherhood: Prayers, Ceremonies & Blessings
Edited and with Introductions by Lynn L. Caruso   5 x 7¼, 272 pp, HC, 978-1-59473-239-3 **$19.99**

Journeys of Simplicity: Traveling Light with Thomas Merton, Bashō, Edward Abbey, Annie Dillard & Others   *by Philip Harnden*
5 x 7¼, 144 pp, Quality PB, 978-1-59473-181-5 **$12.99**; 128 pp, HC, 978-1-893361-76-8 **$16.95**

Keeping Spiritual Balance as We Grow Older: More than 65 Creative Ways to Use Purpose, Prayer, and the Power of Spirit to Build a Meaningful Retirement
by Molly and Bernie Srode   8 x 8, 224 pp, Quality PB, 978-1-59473-042-9 **$16.99**

The Losses of Our Lives: The Sacred Gifts of Renewal in Everyday Loss
by Dr. Nancy Copeland-Payton   6 x 9, 192 pp, HC, 978-1-59473-271-3 **$19.99**

Money and the Way of Wisdom: Insights from the Book of Proverbs
by Timothy J. Sandoval, PhD   6 x 9, 192 pp, Quality PB, 978-1-59473-245-1 **$16.99**

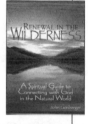

Next to Godliness: Finding the Sacred in Housekeeping
Edited by Alice Peck   6 x 9, 224 pp, Quality PB, 978-1-59473-214-0 **$19.99**

Renewal in the Wilderness: A Spiritual Guide to Connecting with God in the Natural World   *by John Lionberger*
6 x 9, 176 pp, b/w photos, Quality PB, 978-1-59473-219-5 **$16.99**

Sacred Attention: A Spiritual Practice for Finding God in the Moment
by Margaret D. McGee   6 x 9, 144 pp, Quality PB, 978-1-59473-291-1 **$16.99**

Soul Fire: Accessing Your Creativity
by Thomas Ryan, CSP   6 x 9, 160 pp, Quality PB, 978-1-59473-243-0 **$16.99**

A Spirituality for Brokenness: Discovering Your Deepest Self in Difficult Times
by Terry Taylor   6 x 9, 176 pp, Quality PB, 978-1-59473-229-4 **$16.99**

Spiritually Incorrect: Finding God in All the *Wrong* Places   *by Dan Wakefield; Illus. by Marian DelVecchio*   5½ x 8½, 192 pp, b/w illus., Quality PB, 978-1-59473-137-2 **$15.99**

A Walk with Four Spiritual Guides: Krishna, Buddha, Jesus, and Ramakrishna
by Andrew Harvey   5½ x 8½, 192 pp, b/w photos & illus., Quality PB, 978-1-59473-138-9 **$15.99**

The Workplace and Spirituality: New Perspectives on Research and Practice
Edited by Dr. Joan Marques, Dr. Satinder Dhiman and Dr. Richard King
6 x 9, 256 pp, HC, 978-1-59473-260-7 **$29.99**

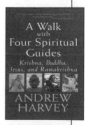

Spirituality & Crafts

Beading—The Creative Spirit: Finding Your Sacred Center through the Art of Beadwork *by Rev. Wendy Ellsworth*
Invites you on a spiritual pilgrimage into the kaleidoscope world of glass and color.
7 x 9, 240 pp, 8-page color insert, 40+ b/w photos and 40 diagrams,
Quality PB, 978-1-59473-267-6 **$18.99**

Contemplative Crochet: A Hands-On Guide for Interlocking Faith and Craft *by Cindy Crandall-Frazier; Foreword by Linda Skolnik*
Illuminates the spiritual lessons you can learn through crocheting.
7 x 9, 208 pp, b/w photos, Quality PB, 978-1-59473-238-6 **$16.99**

The Knitting Way: A Guide to Spiritual Self-Discovery
by Linda Skolnik and Janice MacDaniels Examines how you can explore and strengthen your spiritual life through knitting.
7 x 9, 240 pp, b/w photos, Quality PB, 978-1-59473-079-5 **$16.99**

The Painting Path: Embodying Spiritual Discovery through Yoga, Brush and Color *by Linda Novick; Foreword by Richard Segalman*
Explores the divine connection you can experience through art.
7 x 9, 208 pp, 8-page color insert, plus b/w photos,
Quality PB, 978-1-59473-226-3 **$18.99**

The Quilting Path: A Guide to Spiritual Discovery through Fabric, Thread and Kabbalah *by Louise Silk*
Explores how to cultivate personal growth through quilt making.
7 x 9, 192 pp, b/w photos and illus., Quality PB, 978-1-59473-206-5 **$16.99**

The Scrapbooking Journey: A Hands-On Guide to Spiritual Discovery
by Cory Richardson-Lauve; Foreword by Stacy Julian Reveals how this craft can become a practice used to deepen and shape your life.
7 x 9, 176 pp, 8-page color insert, plus b/w photos, Quality PB, 978-1-59473-216-4 **$18.99**

The Soulwork of Clay: A Hands-On Approach to Spirituality
by Marjory Zoet Bankson; Photos by Peter Bankson
Takes you through the seven-step process of making clay into a pot, drawing parallels at each stage to the process of spiritual growth.
7 x 9, 192 pp, b/w photos, Quality PB, 978-1-59473-249-2 **$16.99**

Kabbalah / Enneagram
(Books from Jewish Lights Publishing, SkyLight Paths' sister imprint)

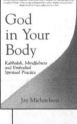

Cast in God's Image: Discover Your Personality Type Using the Enneagram and Kabbalah
by Rabbi Howard A. Addison 7 x 9, 176 pp, Quality PB, 978-1-58023-124-4 **$16.95**

Ehyeh: A Kabbalah for Tomorrow *by Dr. Arthur Green*
6 x 9, 224 pp, Quality PB, 978-1-58023-213-5 **$16.99**

The Enneagram and Kabbalah, 2nd Edition: Reading Your Soul
by Rabbi Howard A. Addison 6 x 9, 192 pp, Quality PB, 978-1-58023-229-6 **$16.99**

The Gift of Kabbalah: Discovering the Secrets of Heaven, Renewing Your Life on Earth
by Tamar Frankiel, PhD 6 x 9, 256 pp, Quality PB, 978-1-58023-141-1 **$16.95**

God in Your Body: Kabbalah, Mindfulness and Embodied Spiritual Practice
by Jay Michaelson 6 x 9, 272 pp, Quality PB, 978-1-58023-304-0 **$18.99**

Kabbalah: A Brief Introduction for Christians
by Tamar Frankiel, PhD 5½ x 8½, 208 pp, Quality PB, 978-1-58023-303-3 **$16.99**

Zohar: Annotated & Explained *Translation & Annotation by Daniel C. Matt;*
Foreword by Andrew Harvey 5½ x 8½, 176 pp, Quality PB, 978-1-893361-51-5 **$15.99**

Spiritual Practice

Laugh Your Way to Grace: Reclaiming the Spiritual Power of Humor
by Rev. Susan Sparks A powerful, humorous case for laughter as a spiritual, healing path. 6 x 9, 176 pp, Quality PB, 978-1-59473-280-5 **$16.99**

Haiku—The Sacred Art: A Spiritual Practice in Three Lines
by Margaret D. McGee Introduces haiku as a simple and effective way of tapping into the sacred moments that permeate everyday living.
5½ x 8½, 192 pp, Quality PB, 978-1-59473-269-0 **$16.99**

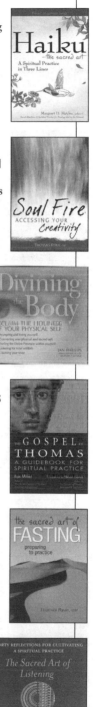

Dance—The Sacred Art: The Joy of Movement as a Spiritual Practice
by Cynthia Winton-Henry Invites all of us, regardless of experience, into the possibility of dance/movement as a spiritual practice.
5½ x 8½, 224 pp, Quality PB, 978-1-59473-268-3 **$16.99**

Spiritual Adventures in the Snow: Skiing & Snowboarding as Renewal
for Your Soul *by Dr. Marcia McFee and Rev. Karen Foster; Foreword by Paul Arthur*
Explores snow sports as tangible experiences of the spiritual essence of our bodies and the earth. 5½ x 8½, 208 pp, Quality PB, 978-1-59473-270-6 **$16.99**

Divining the Body: Reclaim the Holiness of Your Physical Self *by Jan Phillips*
8 x 8, 256 pp, Quality PB, 978-1-59473-080-1 **$16.99**

Everyday Herbs in Spiritual Life: A Guide to Many Practices
by Michael J. Caduto; Foreword by Rosemary Gladstar
7 x 9, 208 pp, 20+ b/w illus., Quality PB, 978-1-59473-174-7 **$16.99**

The Gospel of Thomas: A Guidebook for Spiritual Practice
by Ron Miller; Translations by Stevan Davies 6 x 9, 160 pp, Quality PB, 978-1-59473-047-4 **$14.99**

Hospitality—The Sacred Art: Discovering the Hidden Spiritual Power of
Invitation and Welcome *by Rev. Nanette Sawyer; Foreword by Rev. Dirk Ficca*
5½ x 8½, 208 pp, Quality PB, 978-1-59473-228-7 **$16.99**

Labyrinths from the Outside In: Walking to Spiritual Insight—A Beginner's
Guide *by Donna Schaper and Carole Ann Camp*
6 x 9, 208 pp, b/w illus. and photos, Quality PB, 978-1-893361-18-8 **$16.95**

Practicing the Sacred Art of Listening: A Guide to Enrich Your Relationships and
Kindle Your Spiritual Life *by Kay Lindahl* 8 x 8, 176 pp, Quality PB, 978-1-893361-85-0 **$16.95**

Recovery—The Sacred Art: The Twelve Steps as Spiritual Practice *by Rami Shapiro;*
Foreword by Joan Borysenko, PhD 5½ x 8½, 240 pp, Quality PB, 978-1-59473-259-1 **$16.99**

Running—The Sacred Art: Preparing to Practice *by Dr. Warren A. Kay; Foreword by*
Kristin Armstrong 5½ x 8½, 160 pp, Quality PB, 978-1-59473-227-0 **$16.99**

The Sacred Art of Bowing: Preparing to Practice
by Andi Young 5½ x 8½, 128 pp, b/w illus., Quality PB, 978-1-893361-82-9 **$14.95**

The Sacred Art of Chant: Preparing to Practice
by Ana Hernández 5½ x 8½, 192 pp, Quality PB, 978-1-59473-036-8 **$15.99**

The Sacred Art of Fasting: Preparing to Practice
by Thomas Ryan, CSP 5½ x 8½, 192 pp, Quality PB, 978-1-59473-078-8 **$15.99**

The Sacred Art of Forgiveness: Forgiving Ourselves and Others through God's Grace
by Marcia Ford 8 x 8, 176 pp, Quality PB, 978-1-59473-175-4 **$16.99**

The Sacred Art of Listening: Forty Reflections for Cultivating a Spiritual Practice
by Kay Lindahl; Illus. by Amy Schnapper 8 x 8, 160 pp, b/w illus., Quality PB, 978-1-893361-44-7 **$16.99**

The Sacred Art of Lovingkindness: Preparing to Practice
by Rabbi Rami Shapiro; Foreword by Marcia Ford 5½ x 8½, 176 pp, Quality PB, 978-1-59473-151-8 **$16.99**

Sacred Attention: A Spiritual Practice for Finding God in the Moment
by Margaret D. McGee 6 x 9, 144 pp, Quality PB, 978-1-59473-291-1 **$16.99**

Sacred Speech: A Practical Guide for Keeping Spirit in Your Speech
by Rev. Donna Schaper 6 x 9, 176 pp, Quality PB, 978-1-59473-068-9 **$15.99**
HC, 978-1-893361-74-4 **$21.95**

Soul Fire: Accessing Your Creativity
by Thomas Ryan, CSP 6 x 9, 160 pp, Quality PB, 978-1-59473-243-0 **$16.99**

Thanking & Blessing—The Sacred Art: Spiritual Vitality through Gratefulness
by Jay Marshall, PhD; Foreword by Philip Gulley 5½ x 8½, 176 pp, Quality PB, 978-1-59473-231-7 **$16.99**

Prayer / Meditation

Sacred Attention: A Spiritual Practice for Finding God in the Moment
by Margaret D. McGee
Framed on the Christian liturgical year, this inspiring guide explores ways to develop a practice of attention as a means of talking—and listening—to God.
6 x 9, 144 pp, Quality PB, 978-1-59473-291-1 **$16.99**

Women Pray: Voices through the Ages, from Many Faiths, Cultures and Traditions
Edited and with Introductions by Monica Furlong
5 x 7¼, 256 pp, Quality PB, 978-1-59473-071-9 **$15.99**

Women of Color Pray: Voices of Strength, Faith, Healing, Hope and Courage
Edited and with Introductions by Christal M. Jackson
Through these prayers, poetry, lyrics, meditations and affirmations, you will share in the strong and undeniable connection women of color share with God.
5 x 7¼, 208 pp, Quality PB, 978-1-59473-077-1 **$15.99**

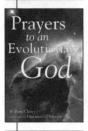

Secrets of Prayer: A Multifaith Guide to Creating Personal Prayer in Your Life *by Nancy Corcoran, CSJ*
This compelling, multifaith guidebook offers you companionship and encouragement on the journey to a healthy prayer life. 6 x 9, 160 pp, Quality PB, 978-1-59473-215-7 **$16.99**

Prayers to an Evolutionary God
by William Cleary; Afterword by Diarmuid O'Murchu
Inspired by the spiritual and scientific teachings of Diarmuid O'Murchu and Teilhard de Chardin, reveals that religion and science can be combined to create an expanding view of the universe—an evolutionary faith.
6 x 9, 208 pp, HC, 978-1-59473-006-1 **$21.99**

The Art of Public Prayer, 2nd Edition: Not for Clergy Only
by Lawrence A. Hoffman, PhD 6 x 9, 288 pp, Quality PB, 978-1-893361-06-5 **$19.99**

A Heart of Stillness: A Complete Guide to Learning the Art of Meditation
by David A. Cooper 5½ x 8½, 272 pp, Quality PB, 978-1-893361-03-4 **$18.99**

Meditation without Gurus: A Guide to the Heart of Practice
by Clark Strand 5½ x 8½, 192 pp, Quality PB, 978-1-893361-93-5 **$16.95**

Praying with Our Hands: 21 Practices of Embodied Prayer from the World's Spiritual Traditions *by Jon M. Sweeney; Photos by Jennifer J. Wilson; Foreword by Mother Tessa Bielecki; Afterword by Taitetsu Unno, PhD*
8 x 8, 96 pp, 22 duotone photos, Quality PB, 978-1-893361-16-4 **$16.95**

Three Gates to Meditation Practice: A Personal Journey into Sufism, Buddhism, and Judaism *by David A. Cooper* 5½ x 8½, 240 pp, Quality PB, 978-1-893361-22-5 **$16.95**

Prayer / M. Basil Pennington, OCSO

Finding Grace at the Center, 3rd Edition: The Beginning of Centering Prayer *with Thomas Keating, OCSO, and Thomas E. Clarke, SJ; Foreword by Rev. Cynthia Bourgeault, PhD* A practical guide to a simple and beautiful form of meditative prayer. 5 x 7¼, 128 pp, Quality PB, 978-1-59473-182-2 **$12.99**

The Monks of Mount Athos: A Western Monk's Extraordinary Spiritual Journey on Eastern Holy Ground *Foreword by Archimandrite Dionysios*
Explores the landscape, monastic communities and food of Athos.
6 x 9, 352 pp, Quality PB, 978-1-893361-78-2 **$18.95**

Psalms: A Spiritual Commentary *Illus. by Phillip Ratner*
Reflections on some of the most beloved passages from the Bible's most widely read book. 6 x 9, 176 pp, 24 full-page b/w illus., Quality PB, 978-1-59473-234-8 **$16.99**

The Song of Songs: A Spiritual Commentary *Illus. by Phillip Ratner*
Explore the Bible's most challenging mystical text.
6 x 9, 160 pp, 14 full-page b/w illus., Quality PB, 978-1-59473-235-5 **$16.99**
HC, 978-1-59473-004-7 **$19.99**

Women's Interest

New Feminist Christianity: Many Voices, Many Views
Edited by Mary E. Hunt and Diann L. Neu
Insights from ministers and theologians, activists and leaders, artists and liturgists who are shaping the future. Taken together, their voices offer a starting point for building new models of religious life and worship.
6 x 9, 384 pp, HC, 978-1-59473-285-0 **$24.99**

New Jewish Feminism: Probing the Past, Forging the Future
Edited by Rabbi Elyse Goldstein; Foreword by Anita Diamant
Looks at the growth and accomplishments of Jewish feminism and what they mean for Jewish women today and tomorrow. Features the voices of women from every area of Jewish life, addressing the important issues that concern Jewish women.
6 x 9, 480 pp, HC, 978-1-58023-359-0 **$24.99***

Dance—The Sacred Art: The Joy of Movement as a Spiritual Practice
by Cynthia Winton-Henry 5½ x 8½, 224 pp, Quality PB, 978-1-59473-268-3 **$16.99**

Daughters of the Desert: Stories of Remarkable Women from Christian, Jewish and Muslim Traditions
by Claire Rudolf Murphy, Meghan Nuttall Sayres, Mary Cronk Farrell, Sarah Conover and Betsy Wharton
5½ x 8½, 192 pp, Illus., Quality PB, 978-1-59473-106-8 **$14.99** Inc. reader's discussion guide
HC, 978-1-893361-72-0 **$19.95**

The Divine Feminine in Biblical Wisdom Literature
Selections Annotated & Explained
Translation & Annotation by Rabbi Rami Shapiro; Foreword by Rev. Cynthia Bourgeault, PhD
5½ x 8½, 240 pp, Quality PB, 978-1-59473-109-9 **$16.99**

Divining the Body: Reclaim the Holiness of Your Physical Self
by Jan Phillips 8 x 8, 256 pp, Quality PB, 978-1-59473-080-1 **$16.99**

Honoring Motherhood: Prayers, Ceremonies & Blessings
Edited and with Introductions by Lynn L. Caruso 5 x 7¼, 272 pp, HC, 978-1-59473-239-3 **$19.99**

ReVisions: Seeing Torah through a Feminist Lens
by Rabbi Elyse Goldstein 5½ x 8½, 224 pp, Quality PB, 978-1-58023-117-6 **$16.95***

The Triumph of Eve & Other Subversive Bible Tales
by Matt Biers-Ariel 5½ x 8½, 192 pp, Quality PB, 978-1-59473-176-1 **$14.99**

Also available: **The Triumph of Eve Teacher's Guide**
8½ x 11, 44 pp, PB, 978-1-59473-152-5 **$8.99**

White Fire: A Portrait of Women Spiritual Leaders in America
by Malka Drucker; Photos by Gay Block 7 x 10, 320 pp, b/w photos, HC, 978-1-893361-64-5 **$24.95**

Woman Spirit Awakening in Nature
Growing Into the Fullness of Who You Are
by Nancy Barrett Chickerneo, PhD; Foreword by Eileen Fisher
8 x 8, 224 pp, b/w illus., Quality PB, 978-1-59473-250-8 **$16.99**

Women of Color Pray: Voices of Strength, Faith, Healing, Hope and Courage
Edited and with Introductions by Christal M. Jackson
5 x 7¼, 208 pp, Quality PB, 978-1-59473-077-1 **$15.99**

Women Pray: Voices through the Ages, from Many Faiths, Cultures and Traditions
Edited and with Introductions by Monica Furlong
5 x 7¼, 256 pp, Quality PB, 978-1-59473-071-9 **$15.99**

The Women's Haftarah Commentary: New Insights from Women Rabbis on the 54 Weekly Haftarah Portions, the 5 Megillot & Special Shabbatot *Edited by Rabbi Elyse Goldstein*
6 x 9, 560 pp, Quality PB, 978-1-58023-371-2 **$19.99***

The Women's Torah Commentary: New Insights from Women Rabbis on the 54 Weekly Torah Portions *Edited by Rabbi Elyse Goldstein*
6 x 9, 496 pp, Quality PB, 978-1-58023-370-5 **$19.99**; HC, 978-1-58023-076-6 **$34.95***

* A book from Jewish Lights, SkyLight Paths' sister imprint

About SKYLIGHT PATHS Publishing

SkyLight Paths Publishing is creating a place where people of different spiritual traditions come together for challenge and inspiration, a place where we can help each other understand the mystery that lies at the heart of our existence.

Through spirituality, our religious beliefs are increasingly becoming a part of our lives—rather than *apart* from our lives. While many of us may be more interested than ever in spiritual growth, we may be less firmly planted in traditional religion. Yet, we do want to deepen our relationship to the sacred, to learn from our own as well as from other faith traditions, and to practice in new ways.

SkyLight Paths sees both believers and seekers as a community that increasingly transcends traditional boundaries of religion and denomination—people wanting to learn from each other, *walking together, finding the way.*

For your information and convenience, at the back of this book we have provided a list of other SkyLight Paths books you might find interesting and useful. They cover the following subjects:

Buddhism / Zen	Global Spiritual	Monasticism
Catholicism	Perspectives	Mysticism
Children's Books	Gnosticism	Poetry
Christianity	Hinduism /	Prayer
Comparative	Vedanta	Religious Etiquette
Religion	Inspiration	Retirement
Current Events	Islam / Sufism	Spiritual Biography
Earth-Based	Judaism	Spiritual Direction
Spirituality	Kabbalah	Spirituality
Enneagram	Meditation	Women's Interest
	Midrash Fiction	Worship

Or phone, fax, mail or e-mail to: SKYLIGHT PATHS Publishing
Sunset Farm Offices, Route 4 • P.O. Box 237 • Woodstock, Vermont 05091
Tel: (802) 457-4000 • Fax: (802) 457-4004 • www.skylightpaths.com
Credit card orders: (800) 962-4544 (8:30AM–5:30PM ET Monday–Friday)
Generous discounts on quantity orders. SATISFACTION GUARANTEED. Prices subject to change.

**For more information about each book,
visit our website at www.skylightpaths.com**